More Seed Bead Stitching

Creative Variations on Traditional Techniques

Beth Stone

KALMBACH BOOKS

Kalmbach Books
21027 Crossroads Circle
Waukesha, Wisconsin 53186
www.Kalmbach.com/Books

Published in 2009
14 13 12 11 10   2 3 4 5 6

Manufactured in the United States of America

ISBN: 978-0-87116-290-8

For Hobbes, I'll miss you forever and for Calvin, who saved me.

And for Ina and Lori, the world's best mom and sister. I love you.

Publisher's Cataloging-In-Publication Data

Stone, Beth, 1960-
  More seed bead stitching : creative variations on traditional techniques / Beth Stone.

    p. : ill. (chiefly col.) ; cm.

  ISBN: 978-0-87116-290-8

1. Beadwork--Handbooks, manuals, etc.
2. Beadwork--Patterns. 3. Jewelry making.
I. Title. II. Title: Seed bead stitching.

TT860 .S76 2009
745.594/2

CONTENTS

MORE SEED BEAD STITCHING:
Creative Variations on Traditional Techniques

THE NEVER-ENDING STORY

Even though *Seed Bead Stitching* was completed, I never stopped playing with beads, and continued creating more variations of tried-and-true beading techniques. As I worked with the beads and moved through a number of stitches and variations, I once again thought I had actually invented some new ones. And as before, I was disappointed to find that I did not. But not one to give up, I gave these new-to-me techniques my own spin.

Throughout this book, you'll find new variations of stitches I introduced in the first book, as well as completely different stitches. Many have basic instructions and illustrations to get you started instead of a full project. I wanted to use as much space here as possible for new work and techniques. For stitches that were not covered in the first book, such as Ndebele herringbone, I wrote detailed instructions and gave you a project or two. Also, because so many of the stitches are three-dimensional, I used bright, contrasting colors and more written instructions and illustrations in order to make sure that each step is clearly explained.

Some projects are tubular and may be a bit more challenging if you're new to beading, but time, practice, and patience will pay off in the end as you learn new techniques.

Mixed with the projects and instructions, you'll find stories about my lifelong bead journey and the evolution of my seed bead work over the past almost three decades. I am constantly amazed at the beaded fabrics that emerge from stitching one bead at a time. I love the excitement of watching project ideas evolve with simple changes in colors and beads.

While the structure of this book is similar to my first, I am excited to give you some new goodies, including seed beading tips and tricks and a chapter about inspiration. There you will find stories from other beaders, some of whom I communicate with on a regular basis and some of whom I have never met. I wanted to give them a chance to help me in this book by imparting some of their bead wisdom. I can't thank them enough.

Some life experiences are such that one vows never to do them again, no matter what (childbirth comes to mind, as does writing my first book). Yet the mind and the body forget the pain and the process over time, as the wonderfulness of the experience begins to reveal itself. I feel that way as I watch my girls grow and thrive, and I feel that way as I hear from my readers who are discovering the joy of seed bead stitching through my published work.

I can't thank you enough for trusting me once again to help guide you in your own seed bead stitching journey. If you are ready, let's get on with it. Enjoy.

Seed beads

When I was about 15 years old, my paternal aunt passed away. She was quite a bit older than my father and had a son quite a bit older than me, so we did not socialize much with them when she was living. Because of this, I did not know that she, too, was a beader. Imagine my surprise and delight when my mother presented me with my inheritance from my aunt: her small bead stash. The beads were stored in little glass medicine bottles and other tiny containers. I set them out on my shelf and loved to look at them. I did not use them. I just looked at them. Believe it or not, I still have them.

Seed beads were limited in color and finish back in 1975, so most of this bead inheritance consisted of 11º or 10º silver-lined beads. I have, of course, expanded my bead collection over the years to rival some bead stores. OK, that may be a slight exaggeration but suffice it to say, I have a lot of beads. And you may, too, if you keep up this highly addictive habit.

Bead stitching, also known as off-loom beadweaving, is the art of creating beaded fabric using only a needle, thread, and assorted beads. The beads most often used to create these stitched fabrics are called seed beads. Seed beads can be found in bead stores, some craft stores, and from online suppliers. There seems to be an endless supply as this art becomes more and more popular. Different bead shapes and sizes create different stitch variations depending on bead placement and order. The main theme throughout this book is: "Don't be afraid to experiment!"

Seed beads are sized by number, and range from 2º (6 mm) to 24º (smaller than 1 mm). The higher the number associated with the bead, the smaller the bead. You will hear bead sizes described as a number, such as "elevens," or see them as a number with a symbol, such as 11º or 11/0 (pronounced "eleven aught"). The most common seed bead size is 11º, but most suppliers carry sizes ranging from 6º (also called E beads) to 15º. Seed beads smaller than 15º are difficult to work with as their holes are tiny. They're also rather scarce—most of these minute sizes are no longer manufactured. I prefer working with beads 6º and smaller.

The most common and highest quality seed beads today are manufactured in Japan or the Czech Republic. These beads are the most uniform and predictable in size, shape, and hole size, plus they're available in an amazing range of colors.

BUYING SEED BEADS

Seed beads from the Czech Republic typically are sold by the hank, a bundle of bead strands (usually 10–12 20-in. strands). Some Charlottes and cut seed beads come in smaller hanks. Japanese seed beads and cylinder beads usually come in tubes or bags and are measured by the gram.

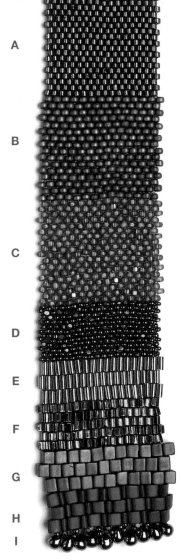

Japanese cylinder beads

Japanese cylinder beads (A) are tubular, with thin walls and large holes that can take many thread passes. They have a consistent size and shape and come in hundreds of colors and finishes. They are most frequently sold in 11ºs, but can also be found in 8ºs and 10ºs. Because cylinder beads are so consistent, they don't require much culling (removing inferior or odd sized beads before beginning a project). Cylinder bead brands include Miyuki Delicas, Toho Treasures, and Toho Aikos. Cylinder beads create a smoother look than you get with rounder seed beads. While cylinder beads are beautiful and easy to use, they don't add much texture to the beadwork.

Japanese seed beads

Japanese seed beads (B) are rounder than cylinder beads, and therefore a good choice for adding texture and visual interest. They come in a range of sizes, but 8ºs, 11ºs, and 15ºs are most common. While not as precisely shaped as cylinder beads, Japanese seed beads are consistently sized, and don't require much culling. A wide range of colors and finishes is available.

Czech seed beads

Czech seed beads (C) are rounder than Japanese seed beads. They are less consistent in size and shape and require more culling. And again, because they are rounder and differ a little in shape and size, they add a bit more texture and visual interest to the work.

Charlottes

Charlottes (D), also called one-cuts or tru-cuts, have a facet on one side that gives a wonderful sparkle. While 13ºs are traditional, they can also be found in 6º, 8º, 11º, and 15º. Use a smaller needle to work with their tiny or irregular holes.

Bugle beads

Bugle beads (E) are long, tube-shaped beads sized from about ⅛ in. (3 mm) to more than 1½ in. (3.8 mm). Bugle beads are made in Japan and the Czech Republic. Each country uses a different numbering system to size the beads, which can be confusing, but in general, the larger the number, the longer the bead. Some bugle beads are twisted for added texture. Bugle beads are notorious for having sharp edges that can cut through beading threads, so you may want to cull beads with broken or sharp ends, or file the rough ends.

Other shapes

Seed beads also come in a variety of additional shapes such as hexagons (F), cubes (G), triangles (H), and drops (I). All of the shapes can be found in several sizes.

Colors and finishes

As if all of these shapes and sizes were not fun enough, seed beads are available in a wide variety of colors and surface finishes. Here are some of the most common.

- Aurora Borealis or AB (1) is a rainbow effect created by applying the finish to hot glass. This rainbow effect is often called "iris" when it's applied to metallic beads.
- Ceylon (2) is a pearl-like finish (sometimes called pearlized).
- Dyed (3) finishes can be found on some Japanese seed beads. This finish will wear off if you don't seal the beads before using them. I try to stay away from dyed beads.
- Luster (4, 9) is a very shiny finish.
- Metallic (5) finish resembles metal. While most metallic finishes are stable, some, like galvanized finishes, may wear off over time.
- Matte (1) beads are usually tumbled or frosted to give them a flat (non-shiny) appearance.
- Opaque (1, 5, 6) beads are solid-colored, nontransparent beads.
- Lined (4, 7, 9) beads are transparent or translucent and have a metallic or opaque coating within the hole.
- Satin (8) finish has a striated look.
- Transparent (7, 9) beads are fairly clear—you can see through them. The color of thread you are using may change the appearance of the bead.
- Translucent (2, 8) beads allow light to pass through them.

Beading thread

The subject of beading thread can get you into a discussion that will never end. Long or short? Waxed or unwaxed? Every beader has a favorite thread and way to use it. You may need to experiment with all of them to find yours.

Silamide thread has been used in the tailoring industry for years. It is a pre-waxed, two-ply, twisted thread that resists fraying. Recently, it has gained popularity with beaders. Silamide is strong and is available in many colors, which is why it's my current favorite.

Single-ply nylon threads are another choice. **Nymo** is a popular brand. It is flat, untwisted, and comes in a range of colors. The thickness is labeled with letters A–F, plus O, OO, and OOO. The closer to the beginning of the alphabet, the thinner the thread, except the Os, which are thinner than A (OOO being the thinnest). The most popular sizes are D and B. Nymo frays if you have to take out mistakes often or if you use a very long thread. Nymo twists while you work with it.

C-Lon was born out of the desire for a product between Nymo and Silamide. C-Lon is offered in two sizes: D (similar in size to Nymo D) and AA (similar in size to Silamide). C-Lon comes in a range of permanently dyed colors and is fray resistant.

SoNo, designed by Japanese master beader Sonoko Nozue, is a cross between Nymo and Silamide. Nozue has developed an improved version called **K.O.** K.O. has a rounder profile and is pre-waxed, making it even more fray-resistant than SoNo. Toho, a competing company, has launched its own similar beading thread, **One-G**.

Fireline is a strong, durable, polyethylene fishing line that is a favorite among beaders. It doesn't stretch, and it's particularly good for stitching with sharp-edged beads, such as bugle beads. The smoke color is almost invisible in most beading projects, while the crystal color can be used with transparent beads (but may look white). Fireline is found in bead stores as well as large sporting goods or fishing stores. Fireline is made in 4 lb., 6 lb., 8 lb., and higher strengths, but 6 lb. and 8 lb. are most appropriate for beadwork. Some Fireline has a thin, dark coating that may rub off on your fingers and lighter-color beads. Run the line through a cloth to remove as much of this coating as possible before beading. Similar to Fireline, **Wildfire** is a thread with a thermally bonded coating which (according to the manufacturer) cannot be pierced with a needle. Like Fireline, it is strong, waterproof, and has zero-stretch. It is available in three colors and two diameters.

Other styles of polyethylene thread include **Power Pro** and **Dandyline**, which are made of polyethylene fibers spun to form thread and then braided or twisted together. These threads are thicker, and therefore not appropriate for bead-work that requires multiple passes through a single bead. (I would not recommend stitching with monofilament fishing lines, as they can become brittle over time and break.)

I have not personally used **Power Pro**, so I turned to seed bead expert Suzanne Golden for her opinion. This is what she told me: "I am a fan of Power Pro fishing line and use it a lot in my work. It's very flexible, does not stretch, and knots easily. Use pliers to flatten the tip of the thread to make it easier to thread the needle. I can use 15 lb. test thread with a #12 needle with no problem."

Thread wax and conditioners

I must confess that I do not use a thread wax or conditioner (because I use Fireline, Wildfire, and Silamide), but I know there are many beaders who can't and won't work without it (these beaders usually use Nymo, SoNo, or C-Lon).

Thread Heaven, created by beader Roni Hennen specifically to make beading easier, is a thread conditioner and protector that both reduces thread tangling, knotting, and fraying, while at the same time protects the integrity of the thread. It adds a static charge to the thread, so it repels itself and is less likely to tangle.

A more traditional thread conditioner is **beeswax**, which usually comes in a bar or round cake. Beeswax adds a fullness to thread that adds tension and helps the beads sit more stiffly when stitched—qualities some beaders find necessary when working certain stitches.

According to Roni, "Using Thread Heaven and wax together can often produce a best-of-both-worlds situation. For example, coating the thread with Thread Heaven, then with wax, will protect it from the acidity and the additional drag of the wax, while the topcoat of wax will impart the additional tension many beaders feel is necessary to work certain types of stitches."

Beading needles

I use English beading needles exclusively in my work. There two kinds: sharp and beading. Sharps are shorter and stiffer than beading needles. Personal preference and comfort will dictate the type of needle you use. The #12 beading needle is perfect for most off-loom beadwork, because it is long and flexible. If you have trouble threading this needle, you may want to try the #11 or #10, but keep in mind that the smaller the needle number, the thicker the needle. Some beadwork (like spiral stitch) requires many passes of thread through each bead, so a thinner needle works better. I have not had any problems using a #12 needle with size 15º seed beads.

Bead dishes and mats

Invest in a few porcelain multicompartment beading dishes. They're great for sorting beads by size and color. Stay away from the plastic look-alikes as they will become very static and your beads will take on a life of their own.

Bead mats, made of a foam-like material, work well on a flat surface. I recommend using a mat-lined tray with sides when beading on your lap.

Scissors and wire cutters

Regular scissors will cut through all of the beading threads except Fireline. For that, use basic wire cutters dedicated to cutting Fireline.

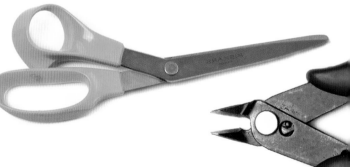

Lighting

There was a time when I could bead in the dark. Then time started catching up with me (and my eyes). While a number of beaders swear by the Ott-lite, I bead with a desk lamp over my shoulder. As long as there is light, I can bead. You will need to figure out what works best for you.

Magnifiers

In the short times since the publication of my first book, I have moved from 2.5 magnifying glasses to progressive lenses, which seem to be working even better. If you are finding that the bead holes and needle holes just don't come into focus any longer, you may just have to visit the eye doctor or drugstore or maybe simply use more light.

Bead vocabulary

Stop bead: This bead is attached to the end of the beading thread (leaving a 10-12 in. (25-30 cm) tail for finishing) to keep the first beads strung from falling off. It's especially useful for beginners. String the stop bead, then go through it again in the same direction. Alternatively, tie an overhand knot around the bead. The stop bead is removed before you work in the tail and finish the piece.

Length of beading thread: Try to begin with the longest piece of beading thread that you are comfortable with (an arm's length is often good). Some projects use a lot of thread (the spiral stitch, for example), while other stitches don't require as much. (See directions for changing thread.)

Thread tail: Leave at least 10–12 in. (25-30 cm) of thread as a tail at the beginning and end of all projects. You will need this thread to attach your closures and clasps.

Working thread: The end of the thread to which your needle is attached.

Knots: The simple overhand knot (bring one end under another and pull) and square knot (go under and pull again) should be all you need.

overhand knot

square knot

Bead soup: I don't know the origin of this term, but it's used to describe a collection of beads left over from other projects. Using bead soup introduces some interesting color, size, and texture combinations. Some people create their own bead soup to get just the right color mix.

Tension: One of the most important aspects of bead stitching is keeping your tension tight and consistent. It may take some practice to get a feel for what the right tension should be. Everyone holds her beadwork differently. With practice and patience, you will find what works well for you.

Surface embellishment: Adding surface embellishment is a fun and easy way to add texture to an otherwise regular surface. I especially like to add this type of dimension to bead-stitched ropes and tubes.

"Finish as desired": There's no one right way to finish a piece of beaded jewelry. You can use metal clasps, buttons, large glass or pearl beads, or my favorite, the beaded loop and toggle. This last technique creates a seamless finish that flows right out of the beadwork. There is a lot of room for creativity in closures—you'll find lots of ideas throughout the book.

To add any closure, use a long tail or secure a new thread in the beadwork (see "Changing threads"), and exit where you want to add the clasp. Depending on the type of clasp you use, you might want to pick up a few beads to create a loop or add some space between the clasp and the beadwork. Otherwise, pick up the clasp, and weave back into the beadwork. Clasps suffer a lot of stress and wear and tear, so be sure to weave through the beadwork and reinforce the join several times.

Changing threads: It's time to start a new thread when you have about 6 in. (15 cm) of working thread left. Thread a new needle with a new thread. Start a few rows back, leave a tail, and weave this new thread through, following the same path as before but avoiding circles or empty spaces. You don't want this new thread to be visible. You may want to tie a few knots around the existing thread as you weave. Come out where the existing thread exits, and resume beading with the new thread. After a few rows, weave in the tails, and trim the thread. When you finish a project, you'll weave the starting and ending tails into the beadwork the same way.

Bead count
three-bead tubular peyote: three beads in each row.
six-bead tubular Ndebele herringbone: three pairs of beads.
two-bead tubular peyote: two beads in each round.
four-bead tubular herringbone, a.k.a. skinny herringbone: two pairs of beads.

BRICK STITCH

Brick stitch naturally decreases at the start and end of each row. If you want each row to have the same number of beads, you'll need to work an increase at either the start or the end of the row.

1. Begin with a ladder of beads (see page 15, Steps 1–5), and position the thread to exit the top of the last bead. To decrease at the beginning of a row, pick up two beads. Sew under the thread bridge between the second and third beads in the previous row from back to front. Sew up through the second bead added, down through the first, and back up through the second bead.

2. For the row's remaining stitches, pick up one bead per stitch. Sew under the next thread bridge in the previous row from back to front, and sew back up through the new bead. The last stitch in the row will be positioned above the last two beads in the row below, creating a decrease.

To increase at the beginning of a row, work as explained above, but start by sewing under the thread bridge between the first and second beads in the previous row.

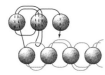

To increase at the end of the row, add a second stitch to the final thread bridge in the previous row.

ZIPPING UP OR JOINING

To join two sections of a flat peyote piece invisibly, match up the two pieces so the end rows fit together. "Zip up" the pieces by zigzagging through the up-beads on both ends.

PEYOTE: FLAT EVEN-COUNT

Pick up an even number of beads (a–b). These beads will shift to form the first two rows.

To begin row 3, pick up a bead, skip the last bead strung in the previous step, and sew through the next bead in the opposite direction (b–c). For each stitch, pick up a bead, skip a bead on the previous row, and sew through the next bead, exiting the first bead strung (c–d). The beads added in this row are higher than the previous rows and are referred to as "up-beads."

For each stitch on subsequent rows, pick up a bead and sew through the next up-bead on the previous row (d–e). To count peyote stitch rows, count the total number of beads along both straight edges.

PEYOTE: DIAGONAL

Diagonal peyote is essentially flat, even-count peyote worked with an increase at the beginning and a decrease at the end of every other row. To work diagonal peyote, start with three rows of flat, even-count peyote. Begin row 4 with an increase by picking up three beads and sewing back through the first of the three beads you just picked up. Work peyote stitch across the row, stopping before you work the last stitch of the row. End the row with a decrease by omitting the final stitch. Turn, and work row 5 in the other direction. Repeat rows 4 and 5 for the desired length.

PEYOTE STITCH: CIRCULAR

Circular peyote stitch is worked in rounds like tubular peyote, but the rounds stay flat and radiate outward from the center as a result of increases (**figure 1** and **photo a**) or using larger beads (**figure 2** and **photo b**).

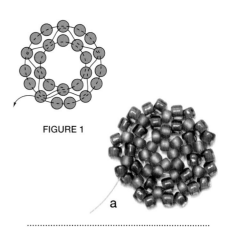

FIGURE 1

a

FIGURE 2

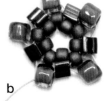

b

While *Seed Bead Stitching* received many really nice reviews, one review mentioned that I did not tell the reader how many beads or exact beads names and colors that I used in individual projects. The fact of the matter is that, for the most part, I don't know. When I make a piece of seed bead stitched jewelry I look through my stash of beads and pick out what I like. I know what you are thinking … just look at the tube and voilà, there is the name. That would work except that a few years ago I transferred most of my beads to those really cute little flip-top containers and did not transfer any names or numbers with them. So, there, my little secret is out. I don't know the color or the number or where I got it.

But really, what fun would there be for you if you use exactly what I used?

Be creative, look at the beads available, and use what you like.

Unless you are buying one of those tiny, tiny tubes of beads, you should be able to re-create most projects here using one large (6 in./30 gram) tube of beads. It's hard for me to give a specific bead count without knowing your size or length preferences.

Finished lengths

A finished length: Bracelet lengths usually range from 6–8 in. (15-20 cm), while necklaces can be 16 in./41 cm (choker length), 18 in./46 cm (sitting just below the collarbone), 20 in./51 cm, 24 in./61 cm, 30 in/76 cm, and longer. Try your piece on from time to time to check the length. Remember adding a clasp will add length to your piece.

I don't pretend to know everything about the world of seed bead stitching. Every time I pick up a needle, thread, and beads, I learn something new. Each mistake I make teaches me not only what not to do, but also teaches me what to do the next time. And over the years I have used many helpful shortcuts and tricks. Here are my favorites.

My top three

1 To add thread, I use a technique I learned from a student years ago. I'd love to credit her, but I cannot remember her name. (If it's you, let me know and I will be sure to add your name to any future printings.)

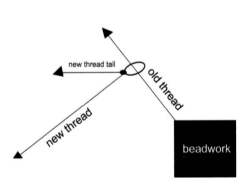

Cut a length of new thread and tie a slip knot into one end, leaving a 6-in. tail. Make the loop very small, and slip the old thread into this newly created loop. Simultaneously, tighten the slip-knot loop while pushing this loop all the way to the beads. Next, pull the short tails of the old thread and new thread. You will hear and feel a tiny

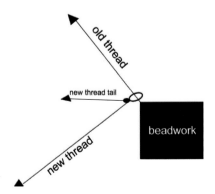

pop. Now, tie one more knot using the two short tails. I have had great success with this technique.

2 When weaving the tail thread back into the work, pass the needle back through several beads, making sure to follow the existing thread paths. Before pulling the thread tight for the last time, leave a small loop of thread, apply a small amount of clear nail polish, let it dry for a few seconds, and then pull tightly. This will force the sticky thread into the beads where it will dry and adhere to the thread already in the beads. As a bonus, clear nail polish will not snap like some instant adhesives will.

3 Throughout this book I will present a number of instructions for tubular variations of stitches. When beginning these stitches try NOT to split the thread with your needle on your initial (base) round of beads. In many cases I will direct you to remove the beginning thread from the bead-work as I guide you through making a seamless connection for a bangle style bracelet.

Tips and tricks from some bead friends

Because I don't pretend to know it all, I put the word out to some wonderful and talented beaders asking if they would share some of their favorite tips. This is what they said:

Lynn Irelan suggests that a bit of beeswax will calm down unruly Fireline.

To seal knots, Lynn suggests swiping the brush from a bottle of clear nail polish over the tip of the beading needle and placing the drop directly on a knot. Be sure to wipe the needle off right away.

Lynn also shares one of my favorite tricks about color. If you are ever perplexed about which colors to put together, browse through magazines (be it fashion, gardening, or whatever) until you come across a color combination that resonates with you. Then clip out a section of the combination and put it in a scrapbook. Fabric swatches and multihued yarns work well, too.

Cissy Gast (aka that beading nut in Katy, Texas) and I met a few years ago via e-mail. She tested some instructions for me for *Seed Bead Stitching* and offered to help me again for this book. We have shared many laughs, many e-mails, a few tears, and a tremendous love for dogs. I love Cissy's beading style and enthusiasm. Cissy is also a very talented painter who uses beading as an escape. "When I'm beading, I know the problems we all have, in one form or another, are still there. However, when concentrating on a bead project, I'm doing just that. Concentrating. It's a great stress reducer."

Cissy also shared one her oft-used tricks: To help stiffen a beaded toggle closure, thinner sculpture wire (1/8-in./3 mm diameter and available in art supply stores) is the best thing to use. It's aluminum, lightweight and flexible. Cut a piece about 1/4 in. (6 mm) shy of the total toggle length. Sand the wire ends smooth with coarse sandpaper. Paint with a coat of clear nail polish. Make the toggle strip slightly larger around than the wire. Zip up the toggle around the wire, adding a 15º rocaille (round seed bead) and 4 mm bead on each end. There will be plenty of room inside the toggle for a couple of passes through the end beads. Snug the thread and exit in the middle of the toggle to add a connection to the necklace or rope. The result is a toggle that is light, strong, and does not collapse with use. One foot (30 cm) of wire will make 10–11 toggles.

Suzanne Golden, a brilliant master beader and new friend, generously shared one of her beading secrets for seamlessly connecting the ends of beaded tubes and spirals: In order to retrace the thread path, she uses white correction fluid to mark the up-beads or the beads that stick out. This lets her keep track of which beads were used to connect the two ends, because once the connection is made the seam is invisible. Suzanne says you can then rerun your thread through the marked beads to secure the joined ends. Knowing that she made a perfect connection makes Suzanne very happy. The little spots of white can be easily removed with a cotton swab and water.

Master right-angle weave beader **Flo Hoppe** has generously shared one of her secrets. To make the beads pop, she uses a contrasting color of bead thread. You can see the difference in these two samples: one with red thread and one with black.

Bead	Diameter in mm	Beads per inch	Beads per centimeter
15° Delica	1.0 mm	21-22	9-10
11° Delica	1.4 mm	19-20	7-8
10° Delica	2.0 mm	13-14	5-6
8° Delica	2.8 mm	9-10	3-4
15° Seed	1.0 mm	25	9-10
11° Seed	1.4 mm	18	7
8° Seed	1.9 mm	13	5
6° Seed	2.5 mm	10	4

Compare finished lengths of seed bead and cylinder bead beadwork with this handy chart.

Pencil boxes from UK company Paper Chase make excellent bead-on-the-go boxes.

Linda Heywood of Beadies Beadwork shares her Delica and seed bead size chart here. You never know when you might need this.

In a lovely handwritten letter, Linda also shared this tip: Use a handy little thread holder to keep your thread untangled. Linda will sometimes use two of these (one for the working thread and one for the long tail thread). When she is working on a project from the center out and runs out of her working thread, she simply unrolls the tail thread and is good to go.

There are so many beading tips and tricks. *Bead&Button* magazine has a page of them in every issue. For example, I shared my idea for using small gift card tins from Michaels craft stores. I line them with a piece of a beading mat (not felt) and use a rubber band for a secure closure. I also found some wonderful larger tins at my local bookstore. They are sold as metal pencil cases but are perfect for beading projects. The two-layer version has a removable tray. Store tubes of beads in the bottom section of the tray and smaller items in the small space under the removable tray. This case has a built-in latch. I must admit that I search for containers to hold on-the-go projects all the time. In my next life I am going to invent the perfect one.

Ndebele herringbone

chapter 1

Ndebele herringbone stitch has gained in popularity over the past several years, and many gorgeous creations are coming from the hands of talented beaders.

A secret: I am not one of those beaders.

While I truly love tubular Ndebele herringbone, I have not yet found myself fully drawn to flat herringbone. Maybe that will change by the time I'm done with this chapter.

NDEBELE HERRINGBONE

When I first saw the word Ndebele, I had no idea how to prounounce it. A friend told me that it sounds like "in the belly." Actually pronounced uhn-duh-BEE-lee, the Ndebele are members of a Zulu people of southwest Zimbabwe. The Ndebele's history is rich; some of its beadwork dates back to the 19th century. Ndebele herringbone looks like little Vs that fit into one another and are stacked in columns. This stitch lends itself well to geometric patterns, which, in original Zulu beadwork, were actually a form of communication. My research also taught me that Ndebele beaders don't use patterns. I guess we have something in common, since I don't work from patterns either. Throughout this book I'll refer to Ndebele herringbone simply as "herringbone."

PROJECT

MATERIALS
• Beading thread
• Size 10 or 12 beading needle
• Japanese cylinder beads

HERRINGBONE SAMPLE

I like to begin using a ladder stitch. Herringbone is worked in pairs, so make sure you start with an even number of beads.

1. Pick up two 11º seed beads **(a)**.

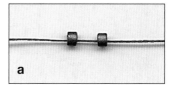

a

2. Pass your needle back through bead #1 in the same direction that you strung it **(b)**. You will be forming a two-bead circle.

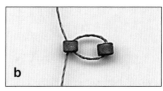

b

3. Pass your needle back up bead #2.

4. Pick up bead #3. Circle back through bead #2 **(c)**.
You will probably notice that the beads don't line up perfectly. This will be taken care of after you add all of the beads you need for the project. Pass the needle back down through bead #3 **(d)**.

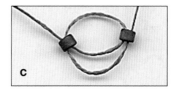

c

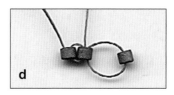

d

5. Continue adding beads in this manner until you have reached your desired width. I used 14 in my sample. Remember that this stitch is worked in pairs. At this point, in order to straighten your bead ladder, pass your needle up and down through all of the beads in the reverse direction. Your working thread and tail thread will now be coming out of the same bead in opposite directions (bead #1) **(e)**.

e

6. With your thread coming out of bead #1, pick up two beads and pass your needle down through bead #2 **(f)**.

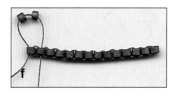

f

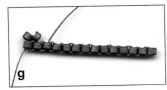

g

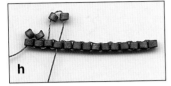

h

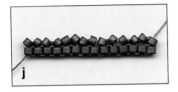

i

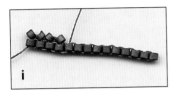

j

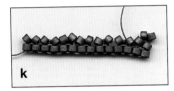

k

7. Pass your needle back up bead #3 **(g)**. Notice how the two beads are sitting slightly crooked. This gives the stitch its herringbone look.

8. Pick up two beads and pass your needle back down bead #4 **(h)**.

9. Pass your needle back up bead #5 **(i)**.

10. Continue as you did in **Steps 8 and 9** four times until you reach the last stitch of the row **(j)**.

11. For this last stitch, pick up two beads. To secure the stitch, you could pass your needle back down into the last bead in the base row as you have been doing, but there is not another bead to go up into. To solve this problem, secure the stitch in a way similar to brick stitch. Instead of passing your needle down through the bead, pass your needle under the thread between the two last beads in the base row. Then pass your needle back up through the last bead of the new row, and you are ready to start row 3. With your needle coming out of the last bead, you are now ready to start the next row.

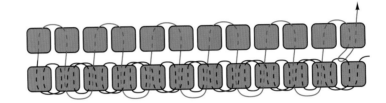

12. Pick up two beads. Pass your needle down through the second bead in the second row and back up the third bead **(k)**. Note that you are passing your needle down and back up only through the beads directly below the row you are stitching.

13. Repeat **Step 10** until you have reached the last stitch in the row, which you will secure as in **Step 11**.

Notice that the stitches all line up in two-bead columns that look like Vs. These two-bead columns are not attached to each other (yet). With your needle coming out between the beads of the V, you add two beads and secure by passing your needle down into the other side of the V. As you create the next stitch you are connecting the columns together. The new stitches that you add in each row are not attached yet. Also, with the ladder start, you may notice a very slight fan out of the beadwork from the base row. This is because of the tilt of the Vs as opposed to the straight base row.

This is just a sample of how to create flat herringbone. You can, of course, continue working until you have a bracelet or choker length and then finish as desired.

An idea!
Try using different sizes of beads to see what happens to the strip of fabric as you progress from row to row.

MATERIALS
- Beading thread
- Size 10 or 12 beading needle
- 15º seed beads
- 11º seed beads
- 8º seed beads

SPUR OF THE MOMENT BRACELET

I named this bracelet "spur of the moment" because I literally designed it as I was writing this chapter. My base row consisted of three bead sizes. After working a few rows, I noticed that the piece started to curve. Wondering what would happen if I reversed the order of the beads, I found that the curve was nicely counteracted. Using big and small beads gives the piece a curvy look along the length. The end result is a bracelet that is stiffer than I anticipated. Hmmm ... the possibilities.

a

b

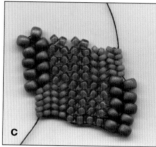

c

1. Make a bead ladder using four 15ºs, four 11ºs, and two 8ºs **(a)**.

2. Work in herringbone stitch for three rows, and you will see how your fabric starts to naturally curve **(b)**.

3. Continue working for two more rows until you have completed five rows.

4. For rows 6–10, reverse the order of your beads **(c)**.

5. Continue reversing the order of your beads after every five rows until you reach your desired length. Finish as desired.

Play with other bead shapes and sizes and different bead orders to create your very own designs!

TUBULAR HERRINGBONE

This stitch produces a supple rope that can be turned into bracelets, necklaces, or lariats. You will work in the round, so there are no turns to worry about. There is, however, a step-up for you to learn, but it is easy to understand.

PROJECT

MATERIALS
- Beading thread
- Size 10 or 12 beading needle
- 11º seed beads in the following colors: opaque orange, opaque green, opaque dark blue, and opaque yellow

HERRINGBONE ROPE

For demonstration purposes, I am going to use a different color for each row so that you can keep track of what I am doing. After you are comfortable with the basics of the stitch, you can follow the row-by-row color instructions to make the bracelet called *Pretty in pastels* on page 20.

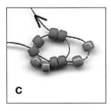
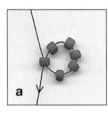
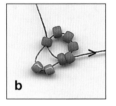
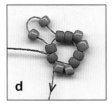

1. Pick up six orange beads. Create a circle by going back through the first bead you strung **(a)**.

2. Pick up two green beads and pass the needle through the next two orange beads **(b)**. Keep in mind that you did this same thing when you worked the flat herringbone project. The only difference now is that you are working around instead of straight across.

3. Pick up two green beads. Pass the needle down the next two beads, just like in **Step 2 (c)**.

4. Pick up two green beads. Pass the needle through the next two orange beads, just like in **Step 3 (d)**.

Here is a simple bracelet made with just one color of seed bead. I used a bold accent color for the toggle.

5. This is the step-up that I referred to at the beginning of this section. To step-up, simply pass the needle through the green bead that is right next to the orange bead your thread is coming out of **(e)**.

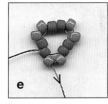

6. With your thread coming out a green bead, pick up two blue beads and pass the needle back down the second green bead of the pair **(f)**.

7. This is the step where you will begin forming the beaded tube. Remember in the instructions for flat herringbone I told you that when you are creating a new row, you are also attaching the bead columns of the previous row? You will be doing the same thing here. Think of the green beads as the tops of the columns as in the flat pattern. You want to attach the second green bead in one column to the first green bead in the next column. To do this you will need to skip over the two orange beads (these are beads from row 1, which means you are done with them) and pass the needle through the first green bead in the next green pair **(g)**. (This is the part of the technique where you will start to pull the beads into a tube, but I suggest that you wait until you have added all of the blue beads.)

8. With your thread coming out a green bead, pick up two more blue beads and pass the needle back though the second green bead of the pair **(h)**.

9. Skip over the next two orange beads and pass the needle through the next green bead. Pick up two more blue beads and secure them by passing the needle down the second green bead of the pair **(i)**.

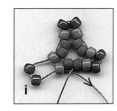

10. You are now ready for the next step-up. Skip over the last two orange beads in the round and pass the needle up into the green bead and the blue bead **(j)**. You are now ready for the next round, and you should be able to pull the beads into the beginning of a tube.

11. With your thread coming out of the middle of the first pair of blue beads, pick up two yellow beads. Pass the needle down the second blue bead of this pair and the first blue bead of the next column **(k)**.

For the purpose of showing you where the first set of yellow beads is placed, I am showing the tube flat or open. The thread that you see between the blue beads will not exist in your piece, since you are pulling your piece into a closed tube.

12. Repeat **Step 11** twice.

13. To step up for the next round, pass the needle through the blue bead and the yellow bead of the next column. Keep trying to gently pull these beads into a tube **(l)**.

Continue stitching the tube until you are comfortable with the stitch.

Pretty in pastels

Now that you are comfortable with tubular herringbone, try combining two different bead sizes to create a bit of texture. For this project, I combined 15º beads in six shades of pastel colors and 11º beads in black and white.

MATERIALS
- Beading thread
- Size 10 or 12 beading needle
- 15º seed beads in six pastel colors (A, B, C, D, E, F)
- 11º seed beads, matte black
- 11º seed beads, matte white

1. Thread a needle with 1½ yards of beading thread and pick up six beads. Stitch 15 tubular herringbone rounds using pastel color A.

2. Stitch five rounds, alternating black and white rounds, beginning with the black beads.

3. Stitch 15 rounds using color B.

4. Stitch five rounds, alternating black and white, beginning with the white beads.

5. Stitch 15 rounds using color C.

6. Stitch five rounds, alternating black and white, beginning with the black beads.

7. Stitch 15 rounds using color D.

8. Stitch five rounds, alternating black and white, beginning with the white beads.

9. Stitch 15 rounds using color E.

10. Stitch five rounds, alternating black and white, beginning with the black beads.

11. Stitch 15 rounds using color F.

Finish the bracelet using a simple loop and peyote-stitched tube.

Textured herringbone tube necklace

This necklace uses a combination of 15º, 11º, 8º, hex, and cube beads. As you work, let your imagination be your guide and have fun with this stitch.

Get the most texture by placing beads of very different sizes next to each other.

Use any combination of bead colors and textures to create your own work of beaded art. Tubular herringbone is very flexible and works well for bracelets as well as necklaces.

TWISTED TUBULAR HERRINGBONE

How about a twist on tubular herringbone? Literally.

I don't know the exact origin of this stitch variation, but if I had to guess, I would say that it started out as a mistake. In regular tubular herringbone, you do a step-up to prepare for the next round by passing your needle into the last bead of the old round and up into the first bead of the newly completed round. To create twisted herringbone, you **do not** pass your needle into that last bead of the old round. You pass your needle only up into the first bead of the newly completed round. And, as you work your way around the tube, there will not be any step-ups at all.

1. Refer to Steps 4 and 5 in the instructions for herringbone rope on pages 18 and 19. Notice in this first picture how you add the last pair of green beads, secure them by passing your needle down into the orange bead, and continue up into the next orange bead **(a)**.

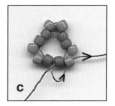

2. Then you continue up into the green bead **(b)**.

3. To begin creating a twisted rope, do not go back up into the last orange bead. Instead, pass your needle directly into the green bead **(c)**.

Remember how I told you in the introduction that these projects will be a bit more complicated? Welcome to the first of "a bit more complicated."

The twist in this technique is very subtle and is not obvious right away. You will have to bead for a couple of inches in order to see it clearly. You may want to use two different bead colors to keep track of where you are, but you don't have to.

For the example below, I used 15° beads in hopes that the twist would appear more quickly.

The twist appeared, of course, but not any faster than it would have if I had used 11° beads. Or 6° beads, for that matter. Still, it needed something more.

I am laughing here, too, but this is how I think and work.

I tried using three different sizes of beads hoping that the twist would just pop out.

MATERIALS
- Beading thread
- Size 10 or 12 beading needle
- 15º seed beads
- 11º seed beads
- 8º seed beads

MEGA TWIST AND TWIRL

"Pop" was an understatement. Mega twist and twirl is a better description. Here's how you do it:

1. Pick up two 15ºs, two 11ºs, and two 8ºs.

2. Follow the instructions for either regular tubular herringbone or twisted tubular herringbone. You will get the same crazy twisted result using either technique. You will notice as you work that you need to bend the tube into an arc in order to neatly and closely attach the columns.

BEAD PLAY

Not one to be satisfied with using different sizes of beads in just one way, I decided to try rotating the order of the beads. In the mega twist and twirl stitch, the same sizes of beads are stacked on top of each other, this technique is a bit different. The result is a very subtle twist, and the beads appear to spiral. This technique can also be done with regular tubular herringbone. Experiment with different combinations of bead sizes and shapes to see what you come up with.

1. Pick up two 15ºs, two 11ºs, and two 8ºs.
2. Using the steps described to create either the regular or twisted tubular herringbone, create your beginning circle of beads by passing your needle through the first 15º.
3. Pick up two 11ºs and pass your needle down the second 15º and up the first 11º.
4. Pick up two 8ºs and pass your needle down the second 11º and up.
5. Pick up two 15ºs and pass your needle down the second 8º.
6. If you are using regular herringbone, pass your needle up the 15º from the first row and the 11º. If you are using twisted tubular herringbone, pass your needle up the 11º only.
7. Continue working in this manner, making sure that you are picking up the beads in a rotating sequence until you reach your desired length. Finish as desired.

MEDALLIONS

There is really no right or wrong way to stitch these. You will notice that quite of bit of peyote stitch is being used, but because this project was born from my experimenting with herringbone, I decided to include it in this chapter. You will need a working knowledge of peyote in order to make these medallions.

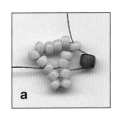
a

1. Beginning with six 11º seed beads, follow **Steps 1–6** from the herringbone rope instructions.

2. Pick up one 8º bead (to fill in the space) and pass your needle up through the first bead of the next bead column **(a)**.

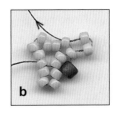
b

3. Pick up two 11ºs and pass your needle down the second bead of the V pair **(b)**.

4. Repeat **Steps 2 and 3** twice. Don't forget to do the step-up to finish the round **(c)**.

c

5. With your thread coming out of the first bead of the V pair, begin the next round by picking up two 11º beads and passing your needle down into the second bead of the pair **(d)**.

6. This time you need to fill in a larger space. Pick up four 11ºs and pass your needle into the first bead of the next V pair. This creates a little frame around the 8º **(e)**.

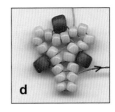
e

7. Repeat **Steps 5 and 6** two more times. Don't forget to do a step-up to complete the round **(f)**.

f

8. Continue adding beads to fill in spaces. Add more 8ºs as the spaces allow. You can also create new Vs along the way as I have done in the next round as shown in the diagram.

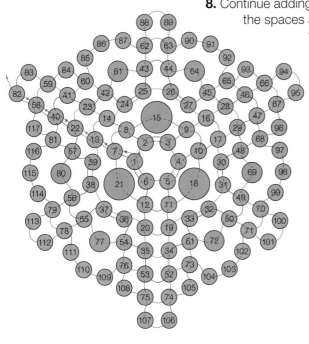

Instead of skipping over those orange beads as in Steps 7–10 of the tubular variation on page 19, I decided to fill in the open space with more beads. This addition of beads kept the piece flat. As I reached a V column on the corners, I added two beads as usual but then again filled in the next space. I continued in this and a similar manner as I expanded the circle (or perhaps you see a star) shape.

| A | B | C | D | E | F | G | H | I | J |

Increasing and decreasing within tubular herringbone

One day, I got a call from a friend asking for specific advice on how to increase within tubular herringbone. This conversation led to this sampler project, which has endless possibilities for increasing and decreasing. I like the colors and textures and could have gone on forever but someone probably wanted dinner or clean clothes so I had to stop. Have fun creating your own sampler rope. In order to create a rope similar to this one, you will need to know the "skinny ropes" version of tubular herringbone (page 83).

These instructions are simply a guide. Where I have stitched two rows, you may like four better. Where I have increased using a particular bead, you may want to change the bead. There is no right or wrong way to do this. The idea is to play with the colors, shapes, and sizes and to experiment with you own ideas.

A
1. Work four-bead "skinny rope" herringbone for four rows using 11º beads.
2. Work the first stitch using the same 11ºs but before you continue up into the next bead pair, pick up an 8º. Work the next stitch and add an 8º before finishing the row. Don't forget that you need to go up into two beads in order to finish and so as not to create a twist in the rope.
3. Repeat **Step 2** but add two 8º s between the stitches.
4. Add three 8ºs between the stitches.
5. To begin the decrease, you will add two 8ºs between the stitches.
6. Add one 8º between the stitches.
7. Work regular herringbone for four rows.

B
8. Work two rows of 8ºs.
9. Work one row of 6ºs.
10. Work two rows of 8ºs.

C
11. Work three rows of 11ºs.

D
12. Work five rows of 15ºs.
13. Add one bugle bead between each stitch.
14. Work one row of 15ºs.
15. Repeat **Step 13**.
16. Repeat **Step 12**.

E
17. This is one of the decreases I mentioned. Instead of picking up two beads for the two stitches in this row, pick up one bead. The added beads will be perpendicular to the regular tubular herringbone work.
18. Add two beads between each of the two single beads just added in the previous row and work regular tubular herringbone for four rows.
19. As in **Step 17**, pick up one bead for each of the two stitches in this row. In order to save some time, let's call this the **single bead stitch**.

20. Work three rows of regular tubular herringbone (RTH).
21. Work one row of single bead stitch with 6ºs.
22. Work two rows of RTH.
23. Work one row of single bead stitch with 8ºs.
24. Repeat **Step 20**.
25. Work one row of single bead stitch with 11ºs.
26. Work four rows of RTH with 11ºs.

F
27. Work one row of single bead stitch with15ºs.
28. Work five rows of RTH with 15ºs.

G
29. Work two rows of RTH with 11ºs.
30. Work one row of RTH with drop beads.
31. Repeat **Steps 29 and 30** twice.
32. Work three rows of RTH with 11ºs.

H
33. Work one row of RTH with 8º hex beads.
34. Work one row of RTH with 6ºs.
35. Work two rows of RTH with 8º hex beads.

I
36. Work two rows of RTH with 11ºs.
37. Refer to **Steps 2–6** for this next section as you will be creating the same type of increase/decrease using all 11ºs. Stitch two rows of RTH.
38. Using single bead stitch, work one row of 11ºs.
39. Work two rows of 11ºs.
40. Steps 2–6 increase/ decrease.
41. Work two rows of RTH with 11ºs.

J
42. Work one row of RTH with bugle beads.
43. Work one row of RTH with 8ºs.
44. Work one row of single bead stitch with bugle beads.
45. Repeat **Step 43**.
46. Repeat **Step 42**.
47. Repeat **Step 43**.
48. Repeat **Step 44**.
49. Repeat **Step 43**.

K
50. Work three rows of RTH with 11ºs.
51. Work one row with 11ºs with an 8º in between each pair.
52. Work one row with 8ºs with an 11º in between each pair.
53. Repeat **Step 51**.

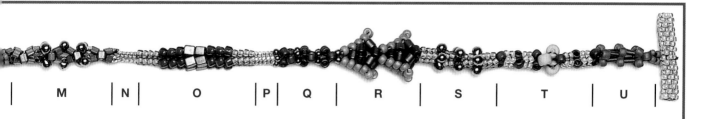

| | M | | N | | O | | P | Q | | R | | S | | T | | U | |

54. Repeat **Step 52**.

55. Stitch two rows of RTH with 11°s.

L

56. Next, use 11°s for the stitch pairs and one 11° in between.

57. Use 11°s for the stitch pairs with two 11°s in between.

58. Use 11°s for the stitch pairs with three 11°s in between.

59. Repeat **Step 57**.

60. Repeat **Step 56**.

61. Stitch three rows of 11°s.

M

62. Stitch one row of single bead stitch with 10° triangles.

63. Stitch one row of RTH with 10° triangles.

64. Repeat **Step 62**.

65. Repeat **Step 63**.

66. Repeat **Step 62**.

67. Stitch one row of RTH with drop beads.

68. Repeat **Step 62**.

69. Repeat **Step 63**.

70. Stitch one row of single bead stitch with drop beads.

71. Repeat **Step 63**.

72. Repeat **Step 62**.

73. Repeat **Step 67**.

74. Repeat **Step 63**.

75. Repeat **Step 62**.

76. Repeat **Step 63**.

77. Repeat **Step 62**.

N

78. Stitch five rows of RTH with 15°s

O

79. Stitch four rows of RTH with 11°s.

80. Stitch three rows of RTH with 8°s.

81. Stitch two rows of RTH with 3 mm cube beads.

82. Repeat **Step 80**.

83. Repeat **Step 79**.

P

84. Stitch five rows of RTH with 15°s.

Q

85. Stitch one row of RTH with 11°s.

86. Stitch two rows of single bead stitch with 8°s.

87. Repeat **Step 85**.

88. Repeat **Step 86**.

89. Repeat **Step 85**.

90. Repeat **Step 86**.

91. Repeat **Step 85**.

R

92. Stitch one row of RTH with 8°s.

93. Stitch one row of RTH with 8°s, with one 8° cylinder bead between each stitch.

94. Stitch one row of RTH with 8°s, with two 8° cylinder beads between each stitch.

95. Stitch one row of RTH with 8°s with three 8° cylinder beads between each stitch.

96. Pass the needle through the cylinder beads again and position it so it is coming out of one of the center cylinder beads. Circle around though the other center cylinder bead so you are tightening the two beads together. These two center beads will be the base for your next cute triangle.

97. Repeat **Step 92**.

98. Repeat **Step 93**.

99. Repeat **Step 94**.

100. Repeat **Step 95**.

101. Repeat **Step 96**.

S

102. Stitch three rows of RTH with 11°s.

103. Stitch one row of RTH with drop beads.

104. Stitch two rows of RTH with 11°s.

105. Repeat **Step 103**.

106. Repeat **Step 104**.

107. Repeat **Step 103**.

108. Repeat **Step 102**.

T

109. Stitch one row of single bead stitch with 8°s.

110. Stitch two rows of RTH with 11°s.

111. Repeat **Step 109**.

112. Repeat **Step 110**.

113. Repeat **Step 109**.

114. Stitch one row of single bead stitch with 6°s.

115. Repeat **Step 114**.

116. Repeat **Step 109**.

117. Repeat **Step 110**.

118. Repeat **Step 109**.

119. Repeat **Step 110**.

120. Repeat **Step 109**.

U

121. Stitch one row of RTH with 8°s.

122. Stitch one row of RTH with short bugle beads.

123. Repeat **Step 121**.

124. Repeat **Step 122**.

125. Repeat **Step 121**.

126. Stitch one row of single bead stitch with 8°s.

127. Stitch two rows of RTH with 11°s.

MATERIALS
- Beading thread
- Size 10 or 12 beading needle
- An assortment of seed beads in different sizes, shapes and colors

If you need a longer necklace, keep working the rope using any of the above techniques, or try something fabulous you thought of as you were working.

You know you did.

I added a toggle bar which I stitched using tubular peyote stitch.

For the blue circle end of the clasp … as I was playing, I came up with a cool little idea I have never seen before. You will learn how to do it in the next project.

FLAT HERRINGBONE WITH FLAIR

MATERIALS:
- Beading thread
- Size 10 or 12 beading needle
- 11º seed beads, purple
- 11º seed beads, green
- 11º seed beads, pink

I enjoy showing the evolution of my work—how one idea can lead to so many others. After using the flat herringbone technique for the blue toggle circle in the previous project, I decided to expand the idea and create a necklace or two. These necklaces (here, and on page 27) have a very subtle difference, but as you can see, the look of the neck straps is quite different. This project, *Flat herringbone with flair*, is made in brown 11º beads and accented with top-drilled pearls. On page 27 you will find the variation, *(Or two)*, that is made in green 11º beads and accented with vertically drilled stone beads. This stitch works up quickly and will take on many different looks depending on the beads you choose.

I use two different 11º beads for the inside beads in the photos to help you keep track of the thread path. For more clarity, I'll use a third color of 11º beads for the outer beads. Then I'll use diagrams to show you how to add the two different types of accent beads. Once you practice the stitch and get the hang of it, try one of these necklaces, or the variations described in the *Bead Play*.

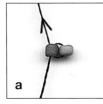
a

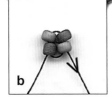
b

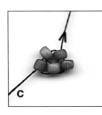
c

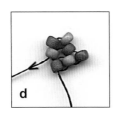
d

e

1. String one purple and one green bead. Pass your needle back through the purple bead so your working thread and tail thread are coming out of the purple bead in opposite directions **(a)**.

2. Pick up one green and one purple bead. Pass your needle back down through the green bead from the first row **(b)**.

3. Pick up one pink bead and pass your needle up through the purple bead in the top row. This positions you to begin the next row **(c)**.

4. Pick up one green bead and one purple bead. Pass your needle down into the green bead from the previous row **(d)**.

5. Pick up one pink bead and pass your needle up through the purple bead on the top row **(e)**.

6. Repeat **Steps 2–5** until you reach your desired length.

You may have to gently push each row of beads in to position. Take care not to push too hard or you may snap your thread. (I hate when that happens!) The beads may not line up correctly until you add the next row. You will see what I mean as you move along with your project.

To add a top-drilled bead:

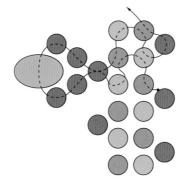

To add a vertical-drilled bead:

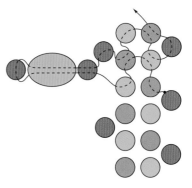

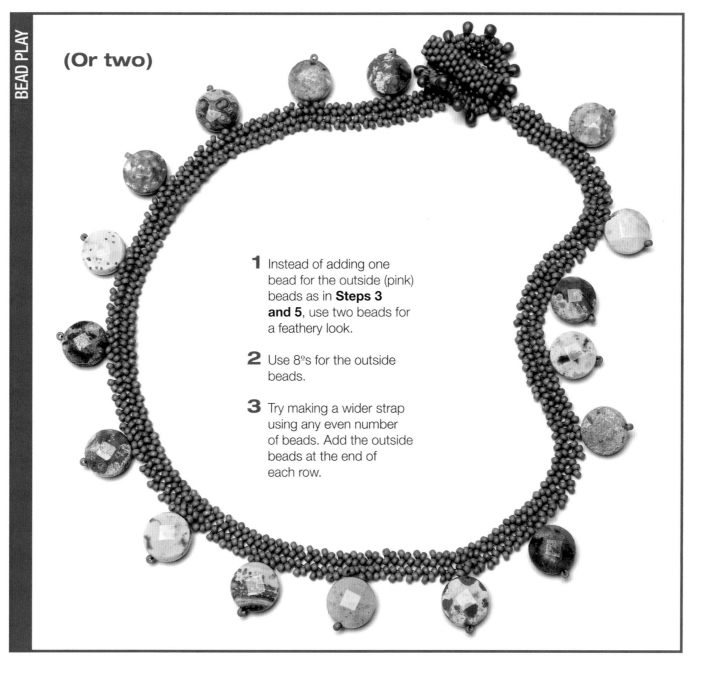

(Or two)

1 Instead of adding one bead for the outside (pink) beads as in **Steps 3 and 5**, use two beads for a feathery look.

2 Use 8ºs for the outside beads.

3 Try making a wider strap using any even number of beads. Add the outside beads at the end of each row.

MATERIALS
- 1 yard beading thread
- Size 10 or 12 beading needle
- 11º seed beads, dark green
- 11º seed beads, light green

INCREASING

a

Increasing within a flat piece of herringbone-stitched fabric is fun and easy. The end result of this technique is a fan shape.

1. Following the instructions for flat herringbone, begin with a ladder of six dark green beads. Work three rows of herringbone **(a)**.

b

2. Pick up two dark green beads and stitch. Before connecting to the next bead column, pick up one light green bead. Now connect to the next bead column **(b)**.

3. Repeat **Step 2 (c)** and finish the row **(d)**.

c

4. Pick up two dark green beads and stitch. Before connecting the stitch to the next bead column, pick up two light green beads. Now connect to the next column **(e)**.

5. Repeat **Step 4 (f)** and finish the row.

d

6. Continue adding beads between the V columns as desired **(g)**, using one additional light green bead per row.

This example uses five light green beads for the increase.

e

f

I will now show you how to create another set of Vs within the increases that you just learned.

g

7. Pick up two dark green beads and work the stitch **(h)**.

h

8. Pick up one light green bead. Skip over the first light green bead in the increase. Pass your needle through the second light green bead in the increase. Pick up two dark green beads. Skip over the third light green bead in the increase. Pass your needle through the fourth light green bead in the increase. Pick up one light green bead and pass your needle up the first bead in next bead column **(i)**.

True confession! I just figured that out right here and now. I have always added these extra Vs without skipping over one bead and then the whole thing ruffles. Now it will continue to lie flat. Don't you just love these types of moments? I do.

Let's continue, shall we?

9. Repeat **Step 7** (working the second stitch of the row) and **Step 8**. Finish the last stitch of the row **(j)**.

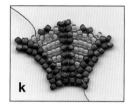

10. Begin the next row by picking up two dark green beads and working the first stitch. Continue by passing your needle through the first light green bead in the row **(k)**.

11. Pick up one light green bead and pass your needle up into the first bead of the new V column **(l)**.

12. Pick up two dark green beads and pass your needle down the second dark green bead of the new V column **(m)**.

13. Pick up one light green bead and pass your needle up the last light green bead before the next V column and then up the first bead of the next V column **(n)**.

14. Repeat **Steps 10–13**. Finish the last stitch of the row **(o)**. Continue working for as many rows as you wish. Add more V columns as desired.

I am not sure what I will use my sample for just yet. What will you do with yours?

Look in Chapter 8 for a variation of this technique. I used this kind of increasing to surround a larger stone bead that finishes a lariat necklace.

Teaser for more herringbone projects and a story, of course ...

While playing with the herringbone medallions, I decided to use only one bead size. The results were this multicolored triangle and this red, white, and black pendant—both of which I embellished with glass beads.

These triangles looked like triangles I had seen some-where else, but mine had a little two-bead opening in the middle. (See the two orange beads half-way down the edges of the multicolored triangle, and the two black beads on the sides of the red, black and white triangle?) I put these aside for a while and started playing with tubular peyote again. It was during my peyote playtime, when I began my project with three beads, that I had one of my "bead awakenings." Instead of filling in the spaces between the beads in the very first round with just one bead, I used two beads (green and black triangle). As I worked, I realized that this is how the previously seen triangles were created.

Until that moment, I thought the triangles had been made in three pieces and then stitched together. I was so excited to have figured this out, but at the same time I had one of my "I guess I did not invent something new" moments (again).

I stayed interested in these triangles and created quite a few of them, but knowing that others were also making them, I knew I had to do something different with them. So I did.

Because most of the triangle is stitched using peyote, you will find them in the peyote chapter, which begins on page 44. But don't skip over there just yet. I'm not quite done.

In the combinations chapter (page 74), you will find a project on combining tubular herringbone with peyote.

I will show you how to add stones or glass beads right into the rope without missing a beat.

In the skinny ropes chapter (page 82), you will find instructions for tubular herringbone with a four-bead start.

Also in the skinny ropes chapter you'll find something really fun: three-dimensional toggle circles! Plain or embellished, these can also be used alone or as chain links.

I am having so much fun. Are you?

Daisy chain

chapter 2

In *Seed Bead Stitching*, I showed you how my favorite childhood stitch, the daisy chain, had grown up by sharing a number of strap type necklaces embellished with stones, glass, and pearls. I also taught you how to layer rows of daisies to create rings. One day while I was stitching a ring using 15° seed beads and tiny pearls, I made a little mistake. This mistake was the starting point of something new for me: my daisy chain circles. These circles can be used as components, as toggle connectors, or linked together to make a bracelet or necklace. So of course, I need to share them here!

DAISY CHAIN

Daisy chain has six beads stitched in a circle, with another bead in the center. The six outside beads shape the petals. Thanks to publishing magic, here are the stitch basics from *Seed Bead Stitching*. To help make things very clear, I am reprising Jeannette Cook's apartment analogy. Imagine the walls, floor, and ceiling of a room. In a six-bead daisy stitch, the side beads are the wall beads, the bead at the top is the ceiling bead, and the bead on the bottom is the floor bead. In a chain of daisy stitches, the stitches share wall beads.

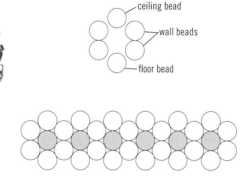

For the daisy circle project, it will be important to know which beads are which in order to understand the variation.

If you are using one 6º bead for the center bead and ten 11º beads for the surrounding beads, your daisy should look like this:

To end one daisy and begin the next, the working thread should be coming down and out the lower of the two "wall" beads.

These two bracelets are composed of multiple daisy chain circles connected with a daisy chain ring. Each daisy chain circle is further embellished with another row of pearls, which adds to the fullness of each circle. Learn how to make the connecting rings in *Bead Play* on page 37.

Here is what I did wrong: You can see that I passed my needle through one of the floor beads. When I began the next daisy, I noticed that the two daisies weren't lining up properly. Instead of taking out the second stitch, I wanted to see what would happen if I deliberately made this mistake again. Much to my surprise, the daisies started to curve. After stitching about 12 or so daisies in the curved chain, I was able to connect the two ends and create a daisy chain circle.

MATERIALS
- Beading thread
- Size 10 or 12 beading needle
- 11º seed beads, red
- 11º seed beads, dark blue
- 11º seed beads, yellow
- 11º seed bead, green
- 6º seed bead, turquoise

DAISY CHAIN CIRCLE

To help simplify these instructions, I suggest you use the same beads and colors as I have. The center bead determines how many surrounding beads you will need to use, so if we are using the same center bead, our bead counts will match. Once you understand how this technique is done, you can use any size center bead you like.

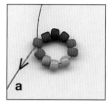

1. String two red beads, one green bead, two yellow beads, two red beads, and three dark blue beads. Create a circle by passing your needle through the first red bead. Your tail thread and working thread will be coming out of the same bead in opposite directions **(a)**.

2. Pick up one 6º turquoise bead. Secure the bead by passing your needle into the opposite lower wall (red) bead **(b)**.

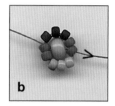

3. To finish the stitch, pass your needle through the two yellow beads. The yellow beads become the new wall beads for the next stitch **(c)**.

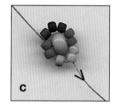

4. Pick up one green bead, two yellow beads, two red beads, and three dark blue beads. Create the next circle of beads by passing your needle through the upper yellow wall bead **(d)**.

5. Pick up one 6º turquoise bead. Secure by passing your needle down into the lower red wall bead on the opposite side **(e)**.

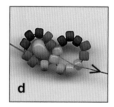

6. To finish the stitch, pass your needle through the two yellow beads **(f)**.

7. Repeat **Steps 4–6** until you have a total of seven daisies.

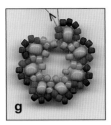

g

8. This last stitch is going to be a bit different. You will attach this eighth and last stitch to the first stitch. Pick up one green bead. Pass your needle up through the two red wall beads from the first stitch **(g)**.

9. Pick up two 11º yellow beads and three 11º dark blue beads. Pass your needle down into the upper yellow wall bead. Pick up one 6º turquoise bead. Complete the stitch by passing your needle down through the lower red wall bead. Your tail thread should be coming up out of the upper red wall bead while the working thread is coming out of the lower red wall bead **(h)**.

Your circle is now complete.

Note: This sample was not intended to be a particular pattern, although as you work, you will see one emerge (with the exception of the spot where the connection is made). I used multiple colors to help you keep track of where you are. If you wish to use this example as a pattern, do the following: In **Step 1**, replace the first two red beads with two yellow beads. In **Step 9**, replace the two yellow beads with two red beads.

You will probably notice that this circle is not very stiff. I recommend that you run your needle through the beads again (following the thread path) to add some stiffness. Be sure to knot the thread a few times for extra security.

h

i

BEAD PLAY

After adding the center bead and securing it into the lower wall bead, instead of continuing through the next two beads (yellow in the above instructions), you can pass through just one of the yellow beads. The end result will be a larger circle that will require 10 or 12 stitches.

Embellishing the circles

To make the circles fuller, you can add another row of 6º beads to the outside of the circle. Use your tail thread if it is long enough; otherwise use your working thread, making sure that the thread is coming out of any upper wall bead.

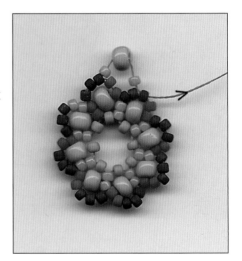

1. Pass your needle through the three dark blue beads. Pick up one yellow bead, one turquoise bead, and one yellow bead. Pass your needle through the third top dark blue bead on the next stitch.

2. Repeat **Step 1** seven times. Secure the thread by passing through a number of beads, tying knots along the way.

Use your circle as a toggle, component, or chain link.

Connecting the circles

For the link bracelets on page 34, each circle is connected with a ring of daisy stitches as explained here. You can also find more projects for using daisy rings in *Seed Bead Stitching*.

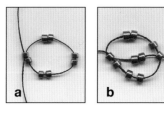

If you wish to use a larger center bead, stone, or pearl, you will need to adjust the number of beads that surround the larger bead (use an even number). Each wall will still consist of two beads. It is the number of beads that will change.

1. Pick up eight beads. Go back through the first bead to create a circle. You will have two beads for each wall, floor, and ceiling **(a)**.

2. Pick up two beads, and pass your needle through the lower wall bead on the opposite side **(b)**.

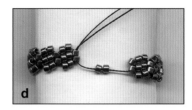

3. Pick up six beads. Create a circle by passing your needle though the upper wall bead above the bead your needle is exiting **(c)**.

4. Repeat **Steps 2 and 3** until the chain is almost the size of a comfortable link for the bracelet. You will be creating a circle with this chain by adding just a tiny bit more to the circumference.

5. The wall on each end of the chain will form the walls of the last daisy, so you will need to add just a floor and a ceiling. Pick up two beads and pass your needle through the two wall beads of the other side **(d)**.

6. Pick up two beads and pass your needle through the top wall bead to make the ceiling **(e)**.

7. Pick up two beads and go through the bottom wall bead on the opposite side **(f)**. You've created an endless ring of daisies.

Inspiration

chapter 3

Forever in my broken heart

I looked up the word "inspire" and was drawn immediately to the archaic definition, "breathing in." When something inspires you, it forces you to breathe in or to breathe life into an idea. When we are struck by something that makes us take notice or say "wow," we are inspired. We all find inspiration in different (or sometimes the same) places that may encourage us to try a new color combination, texture, or style.

In a recent (unscientific) poll on my Web site, bethstone.com, I asked visitors to tell me what inspires them. Of the 63 people who responded 2% said paintings, 6% said fabric, 30% said nature, 37% said other beaders, and 25% said something else. This poll tells me one thing (unscientific as it is) ... beaders like to see the work of other beaders. Personally, looking at beadwork gives me a shot of adrenaline. It gets me excited to bead some more and to continue to inspire others. I do wonder, however, what the 16 "something else" people are inspired by.

Not only can inspiration come from something you see, but it can come from something you feel. In March of 1996 I lost one of the most important people in my life, my daddy. He was it for me. He was handsome and smart, funny and sarcastic, and had a great sense of humor. He was a wonderful husband and father and friend. He loved math and he loved to teach it (especially to me). Shortly after he died I picked up a needle, thread, and beads and tried to lose myself in my work. I did not plan to make anything in

Picture courtesy of
Roche Bobois,
roche-bobois.com.

Nature, or more precisely, the way I feel out in nature, has inspired some of my work. While on vacation a number of years ago in Algonquin Park, Ontario, Canada, I was sitting on the dock with my husband. He was reading and I, of course, was beading. At the time I was doing some strung work with stones, pearls, and sterling silver. The mood of the day was gray. The overcast sky, the dark water, and the white sails all worked in harmony as I created a free-form style necklace using stones that were shades of gray to black, sterling silver, and creamy white freshwater pearls. This necklace then inspired a friend of mine to create a lariat necklace, which made an appearance in *BeadStyle* magazine.

Very recently I became acquainted with Suzanne Golden, who I mention a couple of times throughout this book. She uses a wonderful color palette for her work, which inspired me to stitch some brightly colored skinny Ndebele herringbone circles. You can see more samples of these in the skinny ropes chapter.

My Roche Bobois-inspired bracelet

Lake memories, from Algonquin Park

particular and because I was working in flat peyote at the time, that is the stitch I used. Before I knew it, I had this piece of work in my hands. I called it "Forever in my broken heart," suspended it from a beaded necklace, and gave it to my mom. I did not plan this or pattern it. Believe it or not, it just appeared.

I am also inspired by pictures. I look for colors, patterns, and textures. One day while flipping through the *New York Times* magazine I came upon a picture of living room furniture designed by Roche Bobois. I loved the colors and the patterns and knew there was something beady in my future using this picture as inspiration. I soon had a bracelet on my wrist.

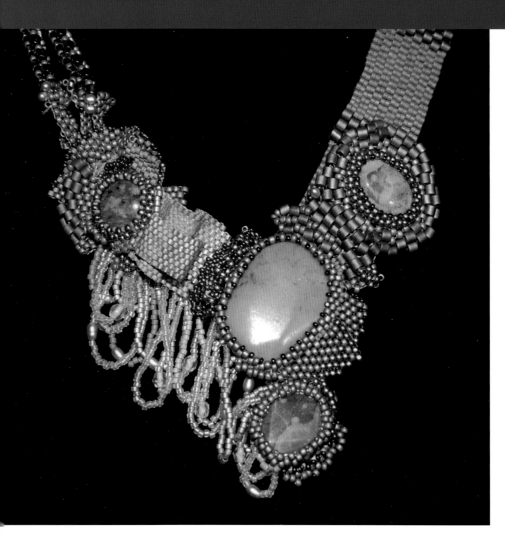

Bobbe Kelley is inspired by nature and memories of shared experiences with her grandmother and mother.

pleased to be able to share it with you here. She begins, "My mother loves neutrals, my paternal grandma loved colors. At times, there was tension between the two women. I was born a week before Christmas, one of the darkest days of the year, made magical by lights. My mother loved all white lights. Though I appreciated their beauty, I harbored secret preferences for the colored lights. When I discovered beading at about age 50, it was the colors of the beads that called to me, that inspired me to begin, and to try something new. The colored beads reawakened the feeling of magic that the colors of the holiday

Suzanne Golden inspired these skinny Ndebele herringbone circles.

During a back and forth e-mail conversation I had with Suzanne about an idea she had, one of us came up with the phrase "creative volleyball," which I define as an ongoing exchange of ideas. I do this a lot with my friend Arlene. We usually end up laughing our heads off and somehow forget about what we were trying to do.

I find it so interesting that given identical images, each of us interprets them so differently. I remember once, years ago, my mom and I did an experiment with bead and wire pins we were making at the time. I gave each of us identical supplies and we went into separate rooms. After about an hour, we came back together and were astonished

at how different our pins were. I wish I had a picture of them to show here but I don't.

I find personal stories fascinating, and enjoy pictures of finished work. So, in addition to some stories from my experience, I'd like to share a few stories from other artists who work in various mediums.

Bobbe Kelley and I have daughters the same age and became friends through our mutual love of beading. Bobbe's work influenced the Nona Necklace (named for her daughter) which was published in *Seed Bead Stitching*. When I was compiling this chapter, Bobbe was one of the first people I called. Her story is beautiful and touching. I am so

Marlene Rackley incorporates colors and textures from her environment in pieces like this pearly charm bracelet.

Kat Olivia kept beading her Jigsaw puzzle pendant, learned from my design, into a lively bracelet.

season used to bring every year, when every thing was so dark. "Now, even in the summer, my experience of beading has inspired me to see nature differently, to notice the myriad shades of green, how it turns to chartreuse, especially in the spring. It was my mother who pointed that out to me one year, after I had my daughters, later in life, when I appreciated the sacrifices of my mother in ways I couldn't have known as a child. I saw more beauty in the brightly lit summer palette than I had noticed before, how a line of purple could run along greens and golds and browns, and thought of how that might work with herringbone, or peyote, or even a Dutch spiral. My grandma

is gone but her colors live on in a painting, an afghan, a quilt, and in me. My mother is still here, and I am so blessed."

I find it so interesting that we are constantly being inspired, even when we may be too young to realize it.

Lynne Irelan, bead artist and teacher, is inspired by jewelry she sees in fashion magazines and catalogs, stores, Web sites, and, of course, bead magazines and books.

Marlene Rackley, a multi-media artist from State College, Penn., shares that, "Inspiration for me comes from the colors all around us, the texture of nature, and just life in general. Sometimes people just need to sit and breathe in their

surroundings and they will be surprised at what they can accomplish as they creating beautiful things."

Allison Berlin, potter, West Bloomfield, Mich., says, "Nature itself is a huge inspiration for me in my ceramics. I have really started looking differently at patterns that occur in leaves, flowers, and seed casings. I am always touching the veins or bumps that are part of these living things. It is amazing what I can find on a nature walk."

Jean Power, London, England, writer, teacher, designer, tells me, "When I first started beading, I discovered that where I placed my decreases and increases enabled me to create different shapes. This revelation

Imagination is the highest kite
one can fly. ~Lauren Bacall

Sandy Tarnopol's watercolors
dance with light and shadows.

SANDY TARNOPOL

has stuck with me ever since and influences much of the work I produce. Although I am often inspired by color schemes, nature, patterns, and other designs, it all changes when I get my beads out and begin to work. Their shapes, colors, and sizes as well as the limitations and peculiarities of each stitch influence which forms actually appear from my needle."

On a recent trip to Denver, Colo., to see some very dear friends, I had the wonderful opportunity to introduce seed beading to their daughter, Melissa Galvin. Melissa, the mother of three gorgeous children, was looking for some-

thing new to do. With my book in hand (she insisted on buying it to support me) and a few beads to get started, I think she found what she was looking for. Over the past year, Melissa has made some lovely pieces for herself as well as gifts for others. When I asked her about what inspires her, she told me, "I usually know what I am about to make, then I play around with different bead combinations, colors, sizes, and stitches until—bingo—it makes sense."

I love the "until it makes sense" part which describes my beadwork perfectly, too.

Beader Delilah Vela contacted me after trying a

pattern idea from *Seed Bead Stitching*. Delilah told me that she is inspired by "... great patterns to follow, color and size of beads, and the individual style of the person I make the jewelry for (I try to add a bead or charm in the work that really fits the person)."

Sandy Tarnopol, acrylic and watercolor artist, Huntington Woods, Mich., writes "I get my inspiration from light and shadows that bring you into the paintings. I also get inspiration from my 10-year-old grandson who asks, Nana are your paintings in the DIA? (Detroit Institute of Arts). If only...."

Laura, photographer, Chicago, Ill., says, "As a

The *Wow* bracelet, by Jennifer Heynen, had me saying "wow" and I couldn't wait to bring her colors and patterns into my stitched work.

Color and nature boldly inspire Jean Power's dimensional beadwork.

photographer, I am inspired by the beauty of nature—macro abstracts, the discovery of unique textures and patterns, and serene landscapes.

Jennifer Heynen, of Jangles, tells me "Nature is where I find inspiration. I am constantly searching for new color combinations to use in my beads and jewelry. I seem to find the best ones come from nature. I have hundreds and hundreds of photos of tide pools. You could say, and my family will tell you, I am a bit obsessed with them. If you look at an urchin or shell and just focus on the colors you will see combinations that you might have never thought of putting

together. I am constantly being surprised by Mother Nature."

Of course, when I saw Jennifer's fun ceramic beads and bracelet, I was inspired to apply her techniques to my beadwork.

Kat Oliva draws energy and inspiration from other artists and their work as well as the patterns of every day life. "When I see color combinations and compositions, my mind starts to find ways to incorporate them into new pieces. When I see something intriguing (a stitch I haven't mastered, a new

technique) I have to try it. The bracelet "Jigsaw Puzzle" is based on a pendant by Beth Stone. I made the pendant and it lay on my work table for about a year. One day I picked it up and started adding here and there and when I finished I had this great bracelet."

I cannot thank these very talented artists enough for allowing me to share their thoughts with you. Take a deep breath or a walk and discover what inspires you.

Peyote

chapter 4

I have a few favorite ways to increase peyote. The first I call diagonal peyote. It results from adding and subtracting columns of beads. I use this technique to create bracelets and neck straps which I leave plain or embellish with stones or pearls. The second increasing technique is to make a forced ruffle or curl by adding more beads than needed into a recessed space. I use these flourishes to create textured effects in sampler necklaces, and I close them to use as toggle clasps. In this chapter, I will show you how to increase and decrease simply by using different sizes of beads. If you know the basics of peyote stitch, this technique will be very easy to do and will create movement or waviness in a bracelet or ring. If you are not familiar with peyote stitch, detailed instructions can be found in *Seed Bead Stitching*.

PEYOTE

Also known as gourd stitch, peyote is one of the first stitches new beaders are introduced to. It is the first beading stitch I learned as an adult, and is the first stitch I taught to my daughters when they were 9 and 10. The flat, even-count version is easy to learn and is a perfect stitch for patterned cuff-style bracelets. I love the look and feel of the finished fabric. I have designed a number of patterns, but like working without a pattern best. Peyote stitch is a great base for adding surface embellishments, and it is fun to play with when working in a free-form style. I often combine peyote with other stitches to create one-of-a-kind pendants. The two- and three-drop versions of this stitch allow for more variations.

PROJECT

MATERIALS
- 2 yards beading thread
- Size 10 or 12 beading needle
- 11º seed beads
- 8º seed beads
- 6º seed beads

EASY BRACELET

For this first bracelet, I used three different bead sizes: 6º, 8º, and 11º. The number of beads in each row does not change, but the changing bead size changes the bracelet's width. Please note that the color of the beads used in the finished bracelet is a bit different than the bead colors used in the instructional photos.

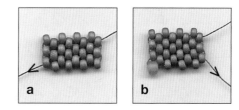

1. Pick up eight 11º seed beads and work in even-count flat peyote for six rows. Count the rows on the diagonal. You will have three beads on each flat side **(a)**.

2. To begin the increase, use one 8º for the first stitch and then finish the row with 11ºs **(b)**.

3. Turn and work peyote for three stitches using 11ºs. For the last stitch of this row, use one 8º **(c)**.

4. Turn and work the next row using 8ºs for the first two stitches and 11ºs for the last two stitches **(d)**.

a

b

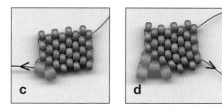

c

d

It is very noticeable how the beads are starting to fan out with each row stitched.

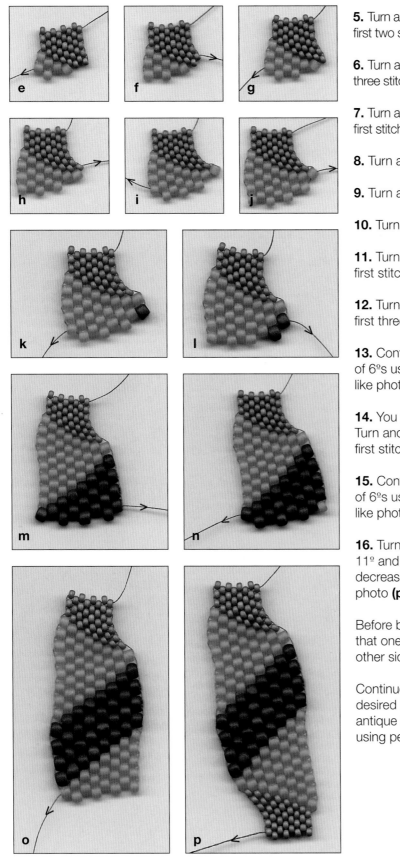

5. Turn and work the next row using 11º's for the first two stitches and 8º's for the last two stitches **(e)**.

6. Turn and work the next row using 8º's for the first three stitches and an 11º for the last stitch **(f)**.

7. Turn and work the next row using an 11º for the first stitch and 8º's for the last three stitches **(g)**.

8. Turn and work the entire row using 8º's **(h)**.

9. Turn and work the entire row using 8º's **(i)**.

10. Turn and work one more row using all 8º's **(j)**.

11. Turn and work the next row using a 6º for the first stitch and 8º's for the last three stitches **(k)**.

12. Turn and work the next row using 8º's for the first three stitches and a 6º for the last stitch **(l)**.

13. Continue working by increasing the number of 6º's used for each row until your piece looks like photo **(m)**.

14. You are now ready to begin the decrease. Turn and work the next row using an 8º for the first stitch and 6º's for the last three beads **(n)**.

15. Continue working by decreasing the number of 6º's used in each row until your piece looks like photo **(o)**.

16. Turn and work the next row by using one 11º and three 8º's. Continue working each row, decreasing the 8º's until your piece looks like photo **(p)**.

Before beginning the next section of 8º's, note that one side of the strip has three 11º's and the other side has six 11º's.

Continue working until you have reached your desired length. I finished my bracelet with an antique button and stitched a square buttonhole using peyote and brick stitch.

Bits and pieces ring

MATERIALS
- 1 yard beading thread
- Size 10 or 12 beading needle
- 11º beads
- 8º beads

This ring can be made in less than an hour and is a perfect project to use up little bits of leftover beads. Oh, that reminds me of a story. I once mentioned something about leftover beads in a published article. A reader got frustrated that I just assumed everyone had leftover beads. She was right. I do assume that most beaders have a tube or two lying around with just a few beads that are waiting to be something. If you don't, please don't take offense. Use whatever you have available. And, if you need to buy new beads for this project, you'll have some left over for the next!

For this ring you will begin the increase right after you pick up the initial four beads.

1. Pick up four 11º seed beads.

2. Begin working even-count peyote using one 8º seed bead and then finish the row with one 11º **(a)**.

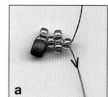

3. Turn and work the next row using one 11º and one 8º **(b)**.

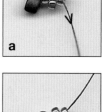

4. Turn and work the next row using two 8ºs **(c)**.

5. Turn and work the next row using two 8ºs **(d)**.

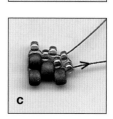

6. Turn and work the next row using one 11º and one 8º **(e)**.

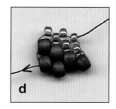

7. Turn and work the next row using one 8º and one 11º **(f)**.

8. Turn and work the next four rows using 11ºs. Your piece should look like photo **(g)**.

To continue, repeat **Steps 2–8** until you reach your desired length. End with an even number of rows.

Zip up (see p. 10) the two ends and weave your threads into the work.

You know that I do not usually give you the names of bead colors because I usually don't know what they are. (Remember, I transfer the beads into flip tops but don't always transfer the names). But this 8º bead color I do know. I found them at a bead show from T & T Trading. The number is F460/denim blue. Yum!

Another way to increase

There are certainly many ways to increase and decrease a piece of beaded fabric. Another way is to add the larger beads all at once in the same row and then decrease the same way. This will cause a rapid flare-out-and-shrink-in as shown here:

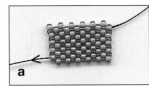

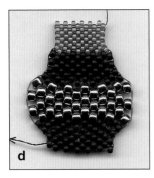

MATERIALS
- 1 yard beading thread
- Size 10 or 12 beading needle
- 15º seed beads
- 11º seed beads
- 8º seed beads

1. Pick up twelve 15º seed beads and work even-count peyote for ten rows. Remember to count on the diagonal. Each of the flat sides will have five beads **(a)**.

I suggest increasing the bead sizes gradually so as not to put too much stress on the thread and beads.

2. Turn, stitch using 11º's for eight rows **(b)**.

3. Turn, stitch using 8º's for six rows. Because there is such a big size difference between 11º's and 8º's, the 8º's will bunch up for the first two rows but will flatten out a bit after the third row **(c)**.

4. Turn and stitch eight rows of 11º's. As you work the first row of the transition, keep in mind that you'll need to pull the beads together tightly. This will force the 8º's into a curved shape, which gives the work a bit of life. Photo **(d)** does not show the curve but you will see it immediately as you are working.

5. Turn and stitch ten rows using 15º's. Again, you will need to pull the beads tightly together, which will cause the 11º's to curve slightly **(e)**.

Continue stitching in this manner until you reach your desired length. Finish as desired.

TUBULAR INCREASES AND DECREASES

It's not a secret that I love tubular stitches. It's also no secret that I love to see how different bead sizes affect the texture of the beadwork.

The bracelet shown here uses 11º taupe beads and 8º black beads.

MATERIALS
- 1½ yards beading thread
- Size 10 or 12 beading needle
- 11º seed beads, blue
- 11º seed beads, red
- 8º seed beads, turquoise

This bracelet is an easy exercise in increasing and decreasing the number of beads used per round in a peyote-stitched bead tube. The thickness of this tube is not dramatically affected by the increases and decreases, but as you work, if you look along the sides of the bracelet, you will see how the beads line up. This can lend itself to unlimited pattern ideas.

1. Pick up three 11º blue beads and create a circle by going back through the first bead you strung in the same direction. Your working thread and tail thread should be coming out the same bead in opposite directions **(a)**.

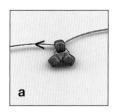

2. Pick up two 11º red beads and secure by passing your needle through the next blue bead in the circle **(b)**.

3. Repeat **Step 2** twice. The working thread and the tail thread should be coming out the same bead **(c)** in opposite directions.

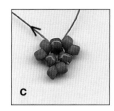

4. Step up by passing your needle up through the first red bead of the first pair of red beads added **(d)**.

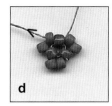

Note: For demonstration purposes the photos show my work flat. The threads you see between the beads will not appear in your work when you pull the beads tightly into a tube.

5. Pick up one 8º turquoise bead and pass your needle down through the next red bead and up through the next red bead **(e)**.

6. Repeat **Step 5** twice. Be sure to end the round by passing your needle through the last red bead **(f)**.

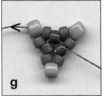

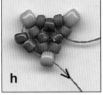

7. Step up to begin the next round by passing your needle through the 8º turquoise bead **(g)**.

There are more instructions for peyote increasing and decreasing in the bonus project titled "Square pillows."

Start tightening your beadwork into a tube. (I will continue to show the tube flat.)

8. Pick up two 11º blue beads and secure by passing your needle through the next 8º turquoise bead **(h)**.

9. Repeat **Step 8** twice. Begin the next round by passing your needle up into the first blue bead of the round.

10. Pick up one 11º red bead. Pass the needle down into the second bead of the pair and up the first bead of the next pair.

11. Repeat **Step 10** twice.

12. Step up by passing your needle up into the red bead.

Continue working the tube. You are alternating adding one bead per stitch and two beads per stitch for the rounds. Add the single bead between the pair of beads added in the previous round. Once you add the single bead and secure it by passing into the next bead, you must then pass your needle up into the next bead before adding the next single bead.

Try experimenting with different patterns, or continue stitching in this manner.

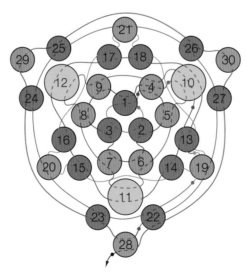

Now that you are comfortable with the basics of the stitch variation, experiment with more bead sizes. This pendant (actually a bracelet wannabe) was made using bead sizes 15º, 11º, 8º, and 6º.

CIRCLES, TRIANGLES, AND SQUARES, OH MY!

MATERIALS
• Beading thread
• Size 10 or 12 beading needle
• 11º seed beads, green
• 11º seed beads, dark blue
• 11º seed beads, yellow
• 8º seed beads, turquoise

"I found I could say things with color and shapes that I couldn't say any other way—things I had no words for." ~Georgia O'Keeffe

I love shapes. Perhaps I was not exposed to enough of them in my wonderful childhood and therefore have a huge affinity for them now. My math mind loves to figure out how to make them and my creative mind loves to figure out what to do with them once they are made. Colors ... patterns ... stripes ... solids ... many ... a few ... attach them ... hang them ... layer them. Where to start?

First, the circles. These circles are made using a four-bead start. The increase expands the circle. Sometimes one bead is added to an open space and sometimes two are added. It really depends on the size of the space. The important part of making these circles is to be consistent in each round. For instance, one round may add just one bead to each space while another round may alternate between adding one bead and then two beads. Your goal is to keep the circle flat. In the beginning of the book, I told you about culling your beads. This is now the perfect time to use some of the inconsistently sized beads to fill in irregularly sized spaces.

To make this easy I am going to use four different colors in this first circle.

1. Pick up four green beads and create a circle by going back through the first bead you strung in the same direction. The working thread and tail thread should be coming out the same bead in opposite directions **(a)**.

2. Working in peyote stitch, add one dark blue bead between each green bead. Your working thread and tail thread should be coming out the same bead in opposite directions **(b)**.

3. Step up through the dark blue bead to begin the next round **(c)**.

4. For this round, fill each space with two yellow beads **(d)**. Note that the thread on the right side is the tail thread. The thread coming out the dark blue bead is the working thread.

a

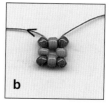
b

c

d

e

5. You need to step up here, but through only one of the yellow beads **(e)**.

6. For this round, you will use the green beads and stitch one bead between every yellow bead **(f)**. Be sure to step up into the green bead to begin the next round.

7. Beginning with two dark blue beads, alternate between filling in the spaces with two then one bead all the way around **(g)**. You will end the round by adding one bead. Step up to begin the next round.

f

8. Add one yellow bead between each dark blue bead. Step up.

9. Add one green bead between each yellow bead. Step up.

10. Beginning with two dark blue beads, alternate adding two and then one bead between each green bead. Step up.

g

11. Add one yellow bead between each dark blue bead. Step up.

12. Add one green bead between each yellow bead. Step up.

13. To finish, add one 8º turquoise bead between each yellow bead **(h)**. Weave your threads into the work to finish. Or, if you are anything like me, don't tie off the ends just yet as you may decide to connect a few of these together, and you will need that thread.

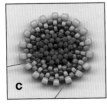

h

NOT DONE YET

These circles are easy to make, but sometimes I just want a little more texture. One day, as I was playing around with these, I wanted to layer them in one piece. I happened to have a long tail thread, so I used it to create another circle right on top of the first. In order to show how this layering is done, I am going to use 11º red beads.

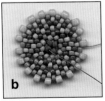

a

1. Thread the tail onto a needle.

2. Notice that the thread is coming out one of the four green beads that you started the circle with. These four beads are going to be the base of the new layer. Imagine that the other beads in the circle do not exist. Pick up one red bead and pass your needle through the second base green bead **(a)**.

b

3. Work three more stitches around the base beads. You are going to step up by passing your needle through the first red bead **(b)**.

4. Using these four red beads as your new base add two red beads between each red base bead. Step up into one red bead only.

c

5. For the next round, add one bead between each red bead. Step up.

6. Add one bead between each red bead. Step up **(c)**.

Add more rounds as desired. Weave in the tails.

MATERIALS
- Beading thread
- Size 10 or 12 beading needles
- 11º seed beads, red
- 11º seed beads, turquoise

TRIANGLES

I have seen beaded triangles like these, but had no idea how they were made. I thought they were constructed by attaching three smaller triangles. One day, while starting a three-bead peyote circle, I had the idea of using two beads instead of just one to fill in spaces for the second round. As I worked each round, I continued stacking the two-bead Vs (as in herringbone) on top of each other and stitched regular peyote to fill in the sides. After a few rounds, I realized that this was how the triangles were made. I began playing with different patterns and bead sizes to see what would happen. I also thought it would be fun to connect a few into a bracelet, and, of course, I needed to layer them. I had an idea one night to use a triangle as a toggle closure, but that meant I needed figure out how to create a triangle with a hole in the center. After a few false starts, it became clear how to make that happen. But first, the basic triangle.

1. Using three turquoise beads, create a bead circle (it actually looks like a triangle) **(a)**.

2. Pick up two red beads and pass your needle through the next turquoise bead **(b)**.

3. Repeat **Step 2** twice. Your working thread and tail thread should be coming out the same bead in opposite directions **(c)**.

4. Step up through the first red bead to begin the next round **(d)**.

Notice the three pairs of red beads look just like the V beads in Ndebele herringbone. Each time you reach one of these Vs, add two beads.

5. With your thread coming out the first bead of the V pair, pick up two turquoise beads and secure them by passing your needle down into the second bead of the V pair **(e)**.

6. Before you can get to the next V pair, you will notice that there is a space that needs to be filled. That is the peyote part of the triangle. Pick up one turquoise bead and pass your needle up into the first bead of the next V pair **(f)**.

a

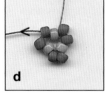
b

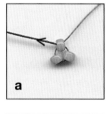
c

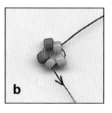
d

e

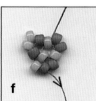
f

g

h

7. Repeat **Steps 5 and 6** twice. Step up through the first bead of the V pair to begin the next round **(g)**. (The thread that looks like it is coming out the right side is actually the tail thread behind the beadwork.)

8. For the next round, add two red beads at each corner and make two peyote stitches between **(h)**.

9. Continue working in this manner, keeping in mind that with each round, the number of peyote stitches increases. Don't be surprised if the triangle becomes a bit concave or convex. You have done nothing wrong. Sometimes—actually, most of the time—it just happens.

There are endless possibilities for patterns using this technique.

Layering the triangle

Refer to the instructions for adding layers to the peyote circles, since layering the triangles is done the same way. The difference is that there are only three base beads to build the layer from, not four.

i

Before beginning the layering, I added a few rounds to the sample triangle.
Note: The thread on the right side is the tail thread. It is coming out one of the three base beads in the center of the triangle **(i)**.

j

10. Remove the needle from the working thread and put it on the tail thread. Using these three beads as the base for the new layer, work three stitches using two beads for each stitch. These are your new V columns. Be sure to step up through the first bead (white in this example) to begin the next round **(j)**.

11. Work this layer the same way you did the base triangle.

Here are examples for layered triangle pendants as well as two layered triangle rings.

Bracelet

This bracelet uses six large triangles and one smaller one for holding the button for the loop-type clasp.

For the orange-outlined triangles:
1. Pick up three turquoise beads.
2. Use the turquoise beads for each V column.
3. Alternate black and white beads for the peyote stitches, beginning with the black beads.
4. After completing eight rounds (nine if you include the beginning beads), stitch two rounds of orange beads.
5. Leave the tail threads for attaching another triangle.

For the blue-outlined triangles:
1. Pick up three green beads.
2. Use green beads for each V column.
3. Alternate black and white beads for the peyote stitches, beginning with the black beads.
4. After completing eight rounds (nine if you include the beginning beads), stitch two rounds of blue beads.

For the green-outlined triangles:
1. Pick up three orange beads.
2. Use orange beads for each V column.
3. Alternate black and white beads for the peyote stitches, beginning with the black beads.
4. After completing eight rounds (nine if you include the beginning beads), stitch two rounds of green beads.

MATERIALS
- Beading thread
- Size 10 or 12 beading needle
- 11º beads in the following colors:
  turquoise
  black
  white
  orange
  green
  blue
- Button or bead

For the small end triangle:
1. Pick up three black beads.
2. Alternate the color of the V columns.
3. Alternate black and white beads for the peyote stitches, beginning with the black beads.
4. Stitch the triangle for eight rounds (nine if you include the beginning beads).
5. Stitch a small bead or button to the center.

Zip up the sections, making sure they are offset throughout.

Stitch a simple loop at the opposite end.

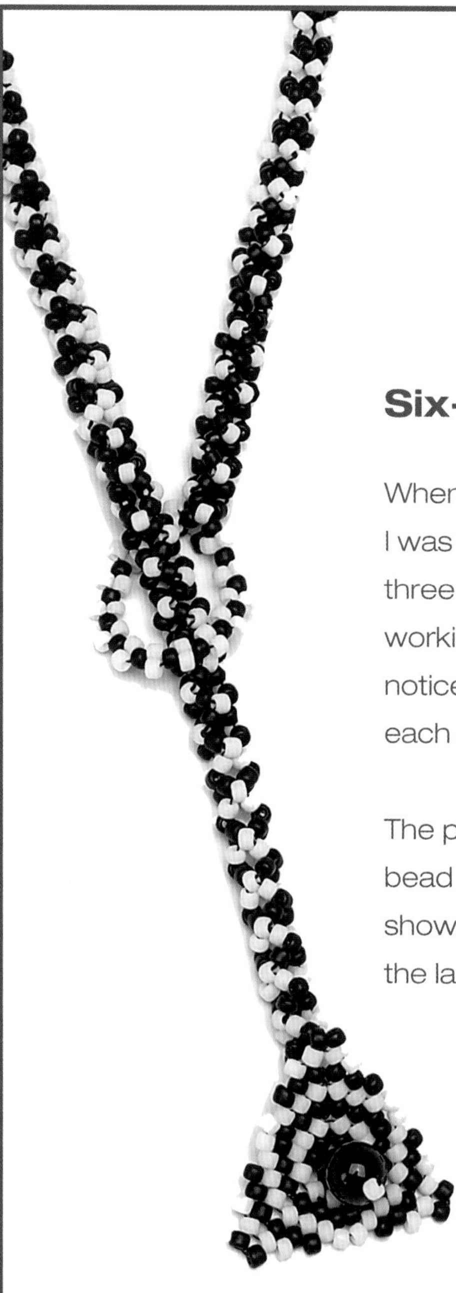

Six-bead start triangle

When I first started making these triangles, I was using a six-bead start instead of the three-bead start I discovered later. When working with a six-bead start, you will notice that there is a two-bead gap on each side of the triangle.

The pendants on page 30 use a six-bead start, as do the toggle clasps shown here. (Instructions for making the lariats are on page 90.)

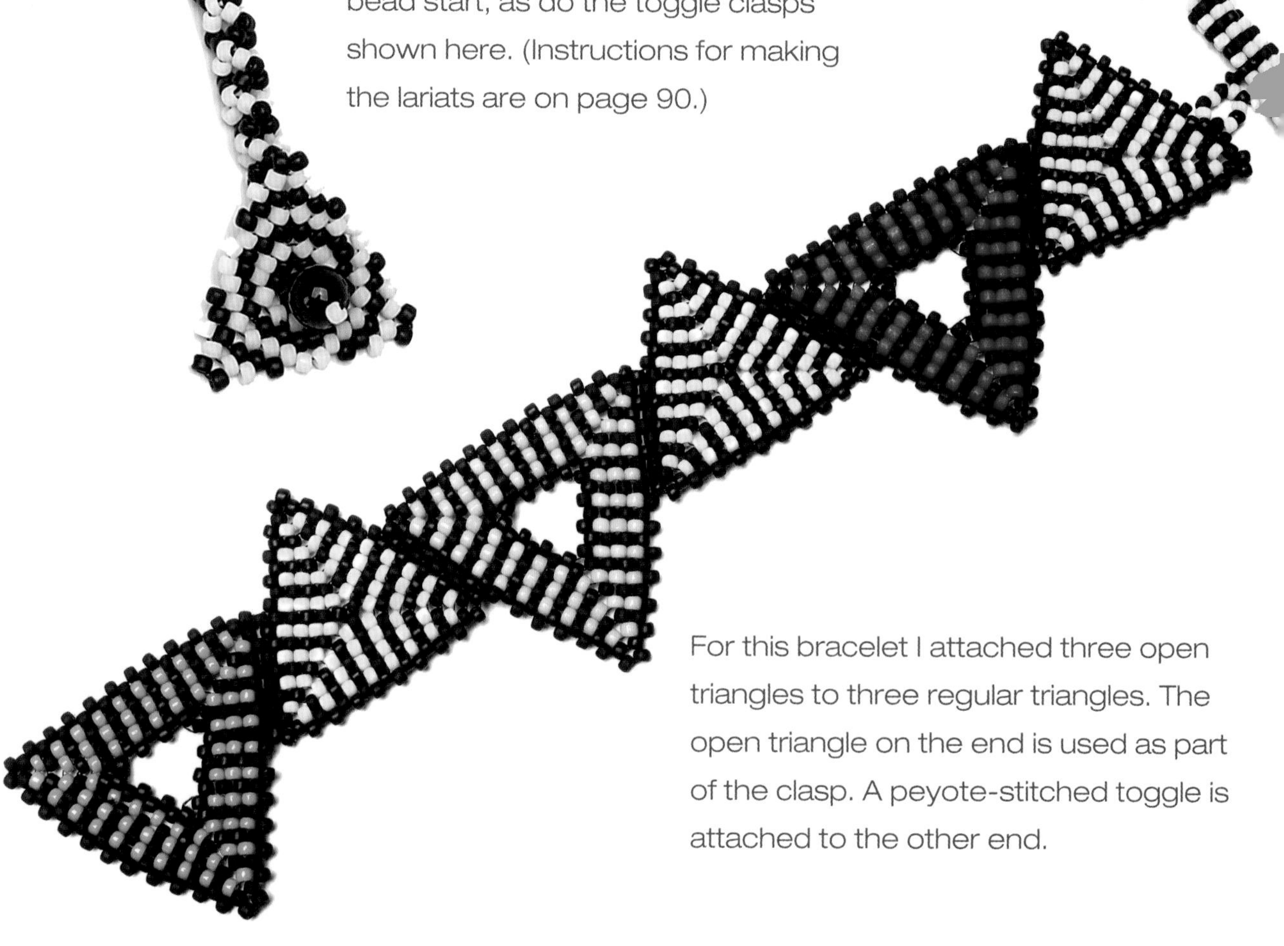

For this bracelet I attached three open triangles to three regular triangles. The open triangle on the end is used as part of the clasp. A peyote-stitched toggle is attached to the other end.

MATERIALS
- Beading thread
- Size 10 or 12 beading needle
- 11° seed beads, black
- 11° seed beads, red

Open Triangles

While working the triangle components bracelet, I had one of my "what if?" thoughts: "What if I made a triangle with an open center and used it as a toggle clasp?" To the drawing board I went. After some trial and error, I figured out that the base row of beads needed to be an odd-number multiple of three (3, 9, 15, 21, 27, etc.). Not much of a surprise given that I was working with a triangle, but nonetheless it took some time to get it right.

1. Pick up 27 black beads and create a circle by passing the needle through the first bead in the same direction you strung it. Your working thread and tail thread should be coming out the same bead in opposite directions **(a)**.

2. Pick up two red beads and pass your needle through the next bead **(b)**.

3. Work in peyote stitch for four stitches using red beads **(c)**.

4. Repeat **Steps 2 and 3** twice **(d, e)**.

5. Step up to begin the next round. The triangle will begin to take shape with the next round of beads.

6. Work this round by picking up two black beads at each of the three corners and working in peyote stitch along the sides. Keep in mind that the number of stitches on each side will increase with each round. Remember to step up at the end of each round **(f)**.

7. Keep working in this manner until you have reached the desired size for your open triangle.

The clasp of this lariat necklace is a stitched open triangle (using triangle beads). It looks great worn in front. The strap is a daisy chain made with 11° and 8° seed beads and the same triangle beads used in the clasp.

SQUARES

Once I conquered the circles and triangles, I was curious about creating squares using the same three- or four-bead circular start.

I had to try this technique a number of times because the squares always seemed to twist instead of lying flat. I am not sure if these will ever be perfectly flat, so if yours are not, don't worry about it. Actually, the slight twist adds some movement and life. And I layered it, too. Did you expect anything less?

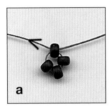

a

1. Pick up four beads and create a circle by passing your needle through the first bead in the same direction you strung it. The working thread and tail thread should be coming out the same bead in opposite directions **(a)**.

b

2. Add one bead between each of the base beads. The working thread and tail thread should be coming out the same bead in opposite directions **(b)**.

c

3. Step up through the next bead to begin the next round. Add two beads between every bead. Step up to begin the next round **(c)**. (Remember, the thread on the right side is the tail thread.)

d

4. Add two beads in each corner V and one bead to fill in the side spaces **(d)**.

5. Continue adding two beads to the corners and one bead to each space on the sides until you reach your desired size **(e)**.

As you work, you may notice a bit of curling. This is normal.

Here is my sample worked for a few more rows. Find out more about layering on the next page.

e

Layering the square

Layering the square is similar to layering the circle and triangle. Just remember the first round for the square uses only one bead between each of the base beads. Subsequent rounds are done as in Step 5 on page 58.

This pendant uses 11º and 8º seed beads and 11º triangles. You will notice that the top square is offset from the bottom layer. In the bottom layer, the first round of beads after the base round uses one bead per stitch and the second round uses two beads per stitch. In the top layer, I used two beads per stitch for the first round.

Try using different sizes of beads to see what results you get.

Spirals

chapter 5

In *Seed Bead Stitching* I created projects using a basic spiral stitch technique. Soon after the book was finished, I came across a Web site owned by Katie Magill. Her instructions for a technique called the double spiral were intriguing.

I was curious to know if she had originated this stitch, and she replied, "I'd love to say that I invented the technique, but I did not. My instructions were probably the first to be published on the Internet as a free tutorial, however."

Katie continued by telling me that she had seen a double spiral posted on an online forum about eight years ago. Katie does not remember the name of the woman but remembers she said, "if you thought about how to do the stitch, you could figure it out." Katie told me that while recuperating from a knee injury she had a great deal of time to try to figure it all out and by trial and error finally came upon a technique that worked. While Katie did not invent this stitch, she has allowed me to share my instruction variation of her double spiral. Thanks, Katie!

SPIRAL STITCH

If you are familiar with regular spiral stitch, you know that you are basically wrapping each stitch (which uses several beads) around a core of beads. Each time you add a stitch, you also add a new core bead, which increases the length of the piece. In the double spiral technique, the addition of core beads is a little different, as you will see in the projects in this chapter. Please note that Katie suggests using an 8º bead for the core in order to accommodate the multiple passes of thread. After some experimenting with 11º beads as the core, I am inclined to agree with Katie. Use the 8ºs.

PROJECT

MATERIALS
- 1½ yards beading thread
- Size 10 or 12 beading needle
- 11º seed beads, black
- 11º seed beads, white
- 8º seed beads, red
- 8º seed beads, black

BLACK, WHITE, AND RED DOUBLE-SPIRAL BRACELET

1. Pick up three 8º red beads, two 11º black beads, one 8º red bead, and two 11º black beads **(a)**.

a

2. Pass your needle back through the three 8º red beads in the same direction you strung them **(b)**.

b

3. Turn the work so that the black/red section is on the right before beginning the next step. Pick up two 11º white beads, one 8º black bead, and two 11º white beads. Create a circle with these beads by passing your needle, once again, through the first three 8ºs from bottom to top. Your working thread and tail thread should be coming out the core beads in opposite directions. Turn the work over again so that the black/red beads are on the left **(c)**.

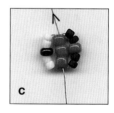

c

4. Pick up one 8º red (core) bead, two 11º black beads, one 8º red bead, and two 11º black beads. To secure the stitch, pass your needle from bottom to top through the top two 8º red beads already in the core and the new 8º you just added. Pull the beads so that these new black/red beads are on top of the previous black/red beads **(d)**.

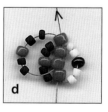

d

5. Turn the work so that the white/black beads are on the left side. Pick up two 11º white beads, one 8º black bead, and two 11º white beads. To secure the stitch, pass your needle from bottom to top through the top three 8º red beads. Pull the beads tight so the new white/black section sits on top of the previous white/black section **(e)**.

e

Note that each time you are on the black/red sections you will pick up a core bead. Each time you are on the white/black sections you will not pick up a core bead.

6. Repeat **Steps 4 and 5** until you reach your desired length.

The double spiral is not any more difficult than that. Make sure that with each stitch you are on top of the previous stitch of the same color.

Experiment with different bead numbers, shapes, colors, and sizes to get very different looks (although intended results may not always occur, as shown).

For this sample, I alternated three black and three white beads. The spiral beads don't really stay put and the look of the spiral tends to disappear. Oh well. It's all part of the fun.

STITCH

CELLINI SPIRAL

The Cellini spiral is a variation of tubular peyote. Master beader Virginia Blakelock is credited with creating this stitch and naming it in honor of 16th century sculptor Benvenuto Cellini.

PROJECT

CELLINI SPIRAL BRACELET

Another beader I count among the masters, Suzanne Golden, uses this stitch beautifully. Suzanne's patterns and color choices (which she calls cirque de soleil) are truly inspirational.

MATERIALS
- 1½ yards beading thread
- Size 10 or 12 beading needle
- 8º seed beads, turquoise
- 11º seed beads, dark blue
- 11º seed beads, orange
- 11º seed beads, yellow
- 15º seed beads, dark turquoise

A gradual increase and decrease in bead sizes forces the spiral, as you will see. Each round begins with the same bead and works the beads in the same order. There is a step up at the end of each round. It will not take you long to notice that the bead you add for each stitch is identical to the bead your thread is coming out. For instance, if your thread is coming out of an 8º purple bead, you will work the next stitch using an 8° purple bead. After playing with this stitch, I recommend using an 11° or 8° bead for the step-up bead.

Here are four spirals. The first spiral uses nine different beads, the second uses five different beads, the third uses three different beads, and the fourth spiral (my personal favorite) uses only two beads for each round.

The instructions are for the five-bead spiral, but keep in mind that a spiral with any number of beads will be constructed the same way. Important: For the first round of beads, make absolutely sure that you do not split your thread. In my version, you will be removing the first round of thread from the beads before attempting to seamlessly connect the ends.

1. Pick up one turquoise bead, one dark blue bead, one orange bead, one dark turquoise bead and one yellow bead. Create a circle by passing your needle back through the turquoise bead. Your working thread and tail thread will be coming out the same turquoise bead in opposite directions **(a)**.

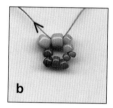

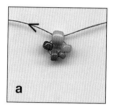

2. Pick up one turquoise bead and pass your needle through the next dark blue bead. Pick up one dark blue bead and pass your needle through the next orange bead. Pick up one orange bead and pass your needle through the next dark turquoise bead. Pick up one dark turquoise bead and pass your needle though the next yellow bead. Pick up one yellow bead and pass your needle through the first turquoise bead. This is the last bead from the base row. Your working thread and tail thread will be coming out the same turquoise bead in opposite directions **(b)**.

3. Step up by passing your needle through the turquoise bead added in this round **(c)**.

4. Pick up one turquoise bead and pass your needle through the dark blue bead that you added in the previous round. Pick up one dark blue bead and pass your needle through the orange bead that you added in the previous round. Pick up one orange bead and pass your needle through the dark turquoise that you added in the previous round. Pick up one dark turquoise bead and pass your needle though the yellow bead that you added in the previous round. Pick up one yellow bead and pass your needle through the turquoise bead that you added in the previous round **(d)**.

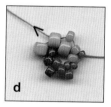

5. Step up by passing your needle through the 8° (turquoise) that you added in this round. Start pulling the beads into a tube **(e)**.

6. Repeat **Steps 4 and 5** until you have reached your desired length. It will take a few more rows of beading to see the spiral begin to take shape. If you are making a bangle bracelet, be sure to make the bracelet large enough around to fit over your hand.

Bangle bracelet with a seamless connection

This will take concentration to complete. You may want to try Suzanne Golden's tips of using correction fluid on the protruding beads on each side to make sure you are connecting the correct beads.

Before connecting the two ends, you need to remove the thread that you used for your base row. If you look at the tail end of your rope, you will see tiny bits of thread peeking out between the first row. Slowly pull the thread out one bead at a time. When your thread is once again coming out the 8º bead (or whichever bead you picked up first), you are done. You can now continue with the connection.

I suggest reading through these instructions before trying to make your first connection.

Make sure that you have completed an entire round of beads and that you have completed the last step up into a turquoise bead.

Hold the two ends as close as possible without losing sight of the beads you need to connect. Look at the how the beads line up, paying close attention to the direction you will be going as you make the connection. I am going to call the end of the tube that your working thread is coming out End X and the other end End Y to help guide you.

For the nine-bead spiral I used beads in this order, 6º, 8º, 11º, 11º, 11º, 15º, 11º, 11º, and 8º.

For this three-bead spiral I used 6º, 8º, and 11º beads.

With your thread coming out the turquoise bead on End X, pass your needle through the turquoise bead on End Y toward the dark blue bead.

Pass your needle through the dark blue bead on End X.

Pass your needle through the dark blue bead on End Y toward the orange bead.

Pass your needle through the orange bead on End X.

Pass your needle through the orange bead on End Y toward the dark turquoise bead.

Pass your needle through the dark turquoise bead on End X.

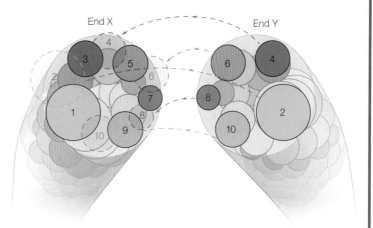

Pass your needle through the dark turquoise bead on End Y toward the yellow bead.

Pass your needle through the yellow bead on End X.

Pass your needle through the yellow bead on End Y toward the turquoise bead.

Pass your needle through the turquoise bead on End X.

Carefully pull the two ends together to complete the seamless connection.

You did it!

And if you didn't, just try again or remember that there is nothing wrong with using a great beaded toggle or button for the clasp.

I don't recommend using a 15° bead next to an 8° or 6° bead, because there will be too much pressure placed on the thread and it may break. I don't think I would use an 11° bead next to a 6° bead either. Try to make your size increases and decreases gradual.

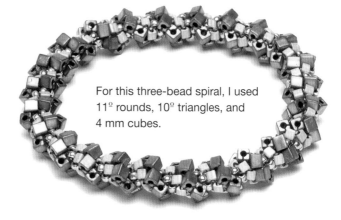

For this three-bead spiral, I used 11° rounds, 10° triangles, and 4 mm cubes.

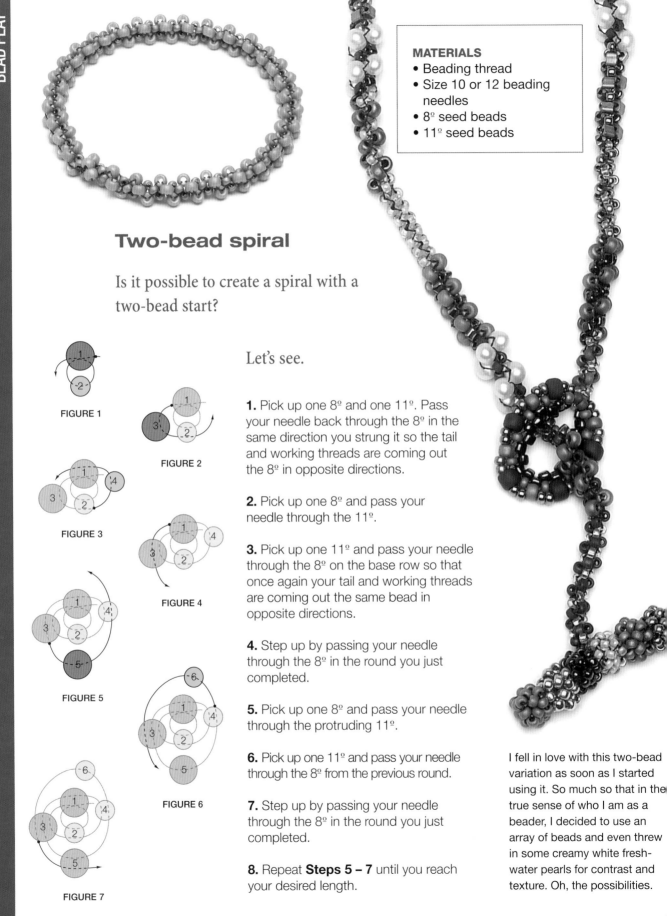

Two-bead spiral

Is it possible to create a spiral with a two-bead start?

FIGURE 1

FIGURE 2

FIGURE 3

FIGURE 4

FIGURE 5

FIGURE 6

FIGURE 7

MATERIALS
- Beading thread
- Size 10 or 12 beading needles
- 8º seed beads
- 11º seed beads

Let's see.

1. Pick up one 8º and one 11º. Pass your needle back through the 8º in the same direction you strung it so the tail and working threads are coming out the 8º in opposite directions.

2. Pick up one 8º and pass your needle through the 11º.

3. Pick up one 11º and pass your needle through the 8º on the base row so that once again your tail and working threads are coming out the same bead in opposite directions.

4. Step up by passing your needle through the 8º in the round you just completed.

5. Pick up one 8º and pass your needle through the protruding 11º.

6. Pick up one 11º and pass your needle through the 8º from the previous round.

7. Step up by passing your needle through the 8º in the round you just completed.

8. Repeat **Steps 5 – 7** until you reach your desired length.

I fell in love with this two-bead variation as soon as I started using it. So much so that in the true sense of who I am as a beader, I decided to use an array of beads and even threw in some creamy white freshwater pearls for contrast and texture. Oh, the possibilities.

As you may have realized by now, my beading mantra is "just play and see where it takes you." In *Seed Bead Stitching* I shared instructions for tubular peyote and even used different bead sizes in the process. After experimenting with the Cellini spiral, I decided to try using two different bead sizes in a different order to see what would happen.

MATERIALS
- Beading thread
- Size 10 or 12 beading needles
- 8º seed beads
- 11º seed beads

First variation

1. Pick up two 8ºs and two 11ºs. Create a circle by passing your needle through the first 8º in the same direction you strung it. The working thread and tail thread should be coming out the same 8º in opposite directions **(a)**.

2. Pick up one 8º and pass your needle through the next 8º in the circle. Pick up one 8º and pass your needle through the next 11º in the circle. Pick up one 11º and pass your needle through the next 11º in the circle. Pick up one 11º and pass your needle through the first 8º in the base row. Your working thread and tail thread should be coming out the same 8º in opposite directions **(b)**.

3. Step up by passing your needle through the first 8º in the row you just stitched **(c)**.

4. Pick up one 8º and pass your needle through the next 8º in the circle. Pick up one 8º and pass your needle into the next 11º in the circle. Pick up one 11º and pass your needle into the next 11º in the circle. Pick up one 11º and pass your needle into the first 8º added in **Step 2 (d)**. You will see that four of the beads protrude. These are the four beads that you will be working with in the next step. As you pull the beads tightly, you will be pulling the beads into the tube.

5. Step up by passing your needle through the very next 8º **(e)**.

Remember that the picture shows the work flat. You will be pulling the beads into a tube.

6. Repeat **Steps 4 and 5** until you reach your desired length.

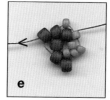

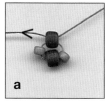

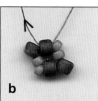

Second variation

1. Pick up one 8º, one 11º, one 8º, and one 11º. Create a circle by passing your needle through the first 8º in the same direction you strung it. The working thread and tail thread should be coming out the same 8º in opposite directions **(a)**.

2. Pick up one 8º and pass your needle through the next 11º in the circle. Pick up one 11º and pass your needle through the next 8º in the circle. Pick up one 8º and pass your needle through the next 11º in the circle. Pick up one 11º and pass your needle through the next 8º in the circle, which is actually the first 8º bead that was strung in the base round. Your working thread and tail thread should be coming out the same bead in opposite directions **(b)**.

3. Step up by passing your needle through the next 8º bead, which is the first 8º bead you added in this new round **(c)**.

4. Pick up one 8º and pass your needle through the next 11º in the circle. Pick up one 11º and pass your needle through the next 8º in the circle. Pick up one 8º and pass your needle through the next 11º in the circle. Pick up one 11º and pass your needle through the next 8º in the circle.

5. Step up by passing your needle through the very next 8º bead.

6. Repeat **Steps 4 and 5** until you reach your desired length.

Third variation

This variation revealed an interesting and unexpected result. While it is not an actual spiral (it's more tubular peyote than spiral), this simple rope version was born out of experimenting with these spiral variations, which is why I am including it here.

At this point you should be familiar enough with creating tubular peyote that written instructions should suffice.

1. Pick up one 8º, one 11º, one 8º and one 11º. Create a circle by passing your needle through the first 8º in the same direction you strung it. The working thread and tail thread should be coming out the same 8º in opposite directions.

Note: For the other spirals and variations, you were instructed to pick up the same type of bead that your thread is currently coming out for each stitch. This variation is done a bit differently.

2. Pick up one 11º and pass your needle through the next 11º in the circle. Pick up one 8º and pass your needle through the next 8º in the circle. Pick up one 11º and pass your needle through the next 11º in the circle. Pick up one 8º and pass your needle through the next 8º in the circle, which is the first 8º strung in the base round. Your working thread and tail thread should be coming out the same bead in opposite directions.

3. Step up into next 11º to begin the next round.

4. Pick up one 11º and pass your needle through the next 8º in the circle. Pick up one 8º and pass your needle through the next 11º in the circle. Pick up one 11º and pass your needle through the next 8º in the circle. Pick up one 8º and pass your needle through the next 11º in the circle.

5. Step up into the next 11º to begin the next round.

6. Pick up one 8º and pass your needle through the next 8º in the circle. Pick up one 11º and pass your needle through the next 11º in the circle. Pick up one 8º and pass your needle through the next 8º in the circle. Pick up one 11º and pass your needle through the next 11º in the circle.

7. Step up into the next 8º to begin the next round.

8. Pick up one 8º and pass your needle through the next 11º in the circle. Pick up one 11º and pass your needle through the next 8º in the circle. Pick up one 8º and pass your needle through the next 11º in the circle. Pick up one 11º and pass your needle through the next 8º in the circle.

9. Step up into the next 8º to begin the next round. Notice how the beads stack straight up onto each other.

10. Repeat **Steps 2–9** until you reach your desired length. Remember to remove the thread from the base round of beads before connecting the ends.

As I work this variation, I am thinking about the color and pattern possibilities. This would lend itself well to a thin reversible bracelet.

Earrings

I love using bead soup for projects like these two-bead spiral earrings with yellow turquoise accents.

Create a section of two-bead spiral stitch. Add a coordinating or contrasting accent bead to one end and an earring finding to the other.

Tah-dah.

Fringe

When I first learned the art of peyote stitch, I, like many other beaders, enjoyed making small amulet bags. Somehow, the bags never looked quite finished without some type of fringe embellishment. As I moved on to other things, I continued to use different fringe techniques on some of my free-form work. Fringe can be simple like the straight technique or more advanced like twisted or branched fringe. Experiment with the different types explained on the next few pages to give your piece of beaded jewelry that extra zing.

FRINGE

When I teach a fringe class, the end result is a sampler piece which the students can use as reference when they are working. Truth be told, once you know how to make fringe, you will probably never forget how to do it, but this sampler is fun to make and keep anyway.

PROJECT

MATERIALS
- Beading thread
- Size 10 or 12 beading needle
- Japanese cylinder beads
- 11º seed beads in several colors
- 8º seed beads
- 6º seed beads

FRINGE SAMPLER

Begin by stitching a piece of even-count flat peyote that is 22 stitches across worked for 14 rows **(a)**.

Circle fringe
Begin the next row with just one peyote stitch. Pick up 14 11º beads. Secure these beads by passing the needle through the next protruding bead (or next bead if you are working on the flat side of the piece) **(b)**.

Here's another way to create this circle fringe. First, work two more peyote stitches. Pick up one cylinder bead and 14 11º beads. Circle back through the cylinder bead and secure by passing your needle through the next protruding bead (or the next bead if you are working on the flat side of the piece) **(c)**.

This alternate way makes a much neater circle that does not tend to twist.

You can also add a larger bead at the bottom of the circle to give the fringe weight and more texture.

Straight fringe
This is probably one of the most common fringe types. Pick up 12 11ºs and one 8º. Skip the 8º and pass your needle back through the 12 11ºs. Secure the fringe by passing your needle through the next protruding bead (or next bead if you are working on the flat side) **(d)**.

Straight fringe with flair
Pick up 12 11ºs, one 8º, one 6º, and one 8º. Skip the 8º, 6º, and 8º beads and pass your needle back through the 12 11ºs. Secure by passing your needle through the next protruding bead (or the next bead if you are working on the flat side) **(e)**.

Hanging loop fringe
Pick up eight color A 11ºs and nine color B 11ºs. Skip the nine Bs and pass your needle back through the eight As. Secure by passing your needle through the next protruding bead (or the next bead if you are working on the flat side) **(f)**.

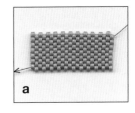

a

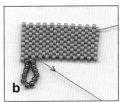

b

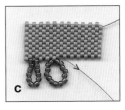

c

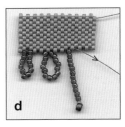

d

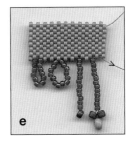

e

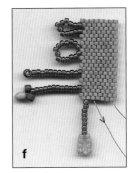

f

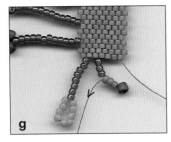

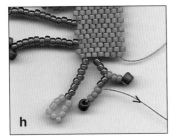

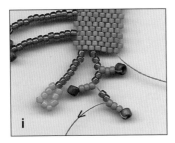

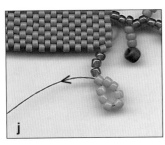

g

h

i

j

k

l

Branched fringe

This fringe has a very organic look, especially when there are a lot of branches.

Pick up three color A 11ºs, three color B 11ºs, and one 8º. Skip the 8º and pass your needle back through the three Bs **(g)**.

Pick up two As, three Bs, and one 8º. Skip the 8º and pass your needle back through the three Bs **(h)**.

Pick up two As, three Bs, and one 8º. Skip the 8º and pass your needle back through the three Bs **(i)**.

To finish the fringe, pass your needle back through the seven As. Secure the fringe by passing your needle into the same or next bead (or next protruding bead). You can, of course, make the fringe as long or as short as you like. This short fringe is simply an example of how to create the branches.

Branched loop fringe

Pick up three color A 11ºs and eight color B 11ºs. Skip seven Bs and pass your needle through the eighth B (the one closest to the branch) **(j)**.

Repeat this process until you have your desired number of branches.

To finish, pass your needle through the As and secure the branch **(k)**.

Branched fringe with flair

This fringe combines the branched fringe and the straight fringe with flair **(l)**.

Staggered (pigtail) fringe

This is a fringe I made up while playing. I call it the pigtail fringe because it curls like a pig's tail. For ease in learning this stitch, I suggest that you use two colors of beads and alternate them.

Pick up 20 beads, alternating the colors. In this example, I used brown and yellow beads, starting with a yellow bead and ending with a brown bead. Skip the last brown bead and pass your needle through all the yellow beads only! Pull the thread tight as you secure the fringe into the next bead (next protruding bead). This will force the fringe beads to curl.

Twisted fringe

This fringe may take a bit of practice, but once you get it, you will be glad you learned. For this example, I strung 20 yellow beads and 20 brown beads so that you can easily see the twist.

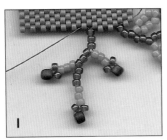

Push the beads all the way up to the work. While holding the beaded sample in one hand, hold the beading thread just past the end of the strung beads in the other. With moistened fingers, start twisting the thread. I like to twist it about 20 times, but you can experiment to find the right twist for you. While keeping the twist in the thread (this is where a third hand would come in really handy), secure the fringe by passing your needle into the next bead in the row (next protruding bead). Keep the twist! Pull the thread tight and, as you let go, the beads will twist around themselves. You may need to try this a couple of times before you get it just right.

As you probably know by now, my theme throughout my books is play! Using the basic instructions for creating fringe as a guide, find and use beads that work well with your piece of bead-stitched jewelry and that add just the right touch. A little or a lot, the choice is yours.

Has the idea of combining different fringe techniques crossed your mind yet?

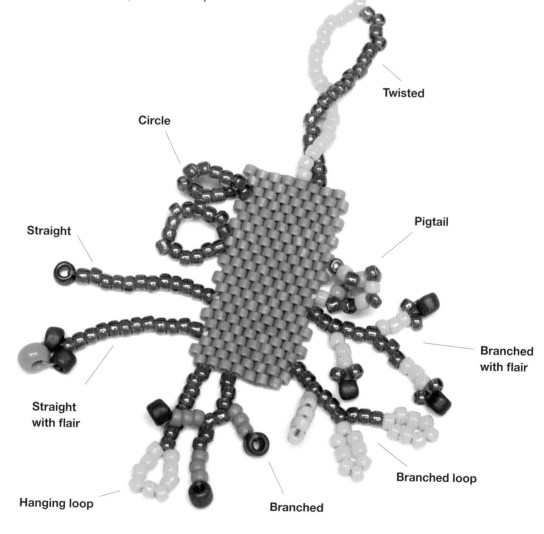

Circle

Twisted

Straight

Pigtail

Branched
with flair

Straight
with flair

Hanging loop

Branched

Branched loop

Combinations

chapter 7

Combining stitches and adding accent beads adds a new dimension to your work. Has it occurred to you yet that I have a very short attention span? It takes a great deal of patience and perseverance for me to make a piece of jewelry that is created using one stitch and one type of bead throughout. I like to play. I like to experiment and I love to see what adding a bead here, or changing a technique there, will do to the look and feel of my beaded fabric or rope. Changing the size, shape, color, or number of beads is something that I just have to do. But changes like these beg the question, "How do I seamlessly blend the techniques?" The answer for me is to add an accent bead and then change the stitch or the pattern. This device gives you many options and helps you create your own work of art jewelry.

PROJECT

MATERIALS
- Beading thread
- Size 10 or 12 beading needle
- 11° seed beads
- Glass or stone accent beads with holes large enough for five thread passes

ADDING ACCENT BEADS TO SKINNY TUBULAR HERRINGBONE

This necklace was created after a friend handed me some black, white, and red art glass and said, "Do something with these." At the time I was working on some new herringbone pieces, so herringbone was my stitch of choice. I knew that I wanted to use tubular herringbone, but I was not sure just how to incorporate the glass beads so that they looked like they belonged. I quickly figured out a relatively easy technique.

1. Create a 10-row herringbone skinny rope (see Chapter 8).

If you look at the working end of your rope, you will see four beads. The thread is coming out one of them. If you were to make a new stitch you would pick up two beads and secure them by passing your needle down through the second bead of the V pair. Well, you will do just that, but first, pick up an accent bead. (In the diagrams, the circles on the left are the existing beads, the blue circle is the accent bead, and the circles on the right are the new beads.)

2. With your needle coming out bead #1, pick up one accent bead and two seed beads, #2 and #3.

3. Pass your needle back down through the accent bead and bead #4 to secure.

4. Pass your needle up through bead #5.

5. Pass your needle up through the accent bead.

6. Pick up two seed beads (#6 and #7).

7. Pass your needle back down through the accent bead and #8.

8. Pass your needle up through #1.

9. Pass your needle up through the accent bead and through one of the four beads just added.

10. Work herringbone for a number of rows using any beads you wish.

11. Add accent beads as desired along the length of the necklace. Finish as desired.

PROJECT

MATERIALS:
- Beading thread
- Size 10 or 12 beading needle
- 11º seed beads
- Glass or stone accent beads

MULTISTITCH, MULTISTONE NECKLACE

Here are instructions for adding accent beads between different tubular stitches.

Adding an accent bead to three-bead tubular peyote

With your needle coming out bead #1, pick up an accent bead and bead #2.

Pass your needle back through the accent bead and through bead #3.

Pass your needle back through the accent bead and pick up bead #4.

Pass your needle back through the accent bead and through bead #5.

Pass your needle back through the accent bead and pick up bead #6.

Pass your needle back through the accent bead and through bead #1.

Pass your needle back through the accent bead and through bead #2.

Continue with three-bead tubular peyote.

This necklace is made using multiple tubular stitches and an eclectic mix of stones. Included here are six-bead herringbone, basic spiral, peyote, embellished peyote, four-bead (skinny) herringbone, and a stitch I call Fabulous, explained in *Seed Bead Stitching*.

Adding an accent bead between three-bead peyote and skinny Ndebele herringbone

With your needle coming out bead #1, pick up the accent bead and beads #2 and #3.

Pass your needle back through the accent bead and through bead #4.

Pass your needle back through the accent bead and pick up #5 and #6.

Pass your needle back through the accent bead and through bead #7.

Pass your needle back through the accent bead and through bead #2.

Continue with skinny herringbone.

 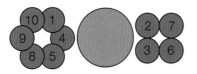

Adding an accent bead between skinny herringbone and three-bead Peyote

With your needle coming out bead #1, pick up an accent bead and bead #2.

Pass your needle back through the accent bead, down bead #3, and up bead #4.

Pass your needle back through the accent bead and pick up bead #5.

Pass your needle back through the accent bead, down bead #6, and up bead #1.

Pass your needle back through the accent bead and pick up bead #7.

Note: You may want to secure bead #7 by passing your needle back through the accent bead and through beads #3 and #4 or even diagonally through beads #3 and #6.

Pass your needle back through the accent bead and bead #2.

Continue with three-bead peyote.

Adding an accent bead between six-bead herringbone and four-bead herringbone

With your thread coming out bead #1, pick up an accent bead and beads #2 and #3.

Pass your needle back through the accent bead, down bead #4, and up bead #5.

Pass your needle back through the accent bead and pick up beads #6 and #7.

Pass your needle back through the accent bead, down bead #8, and up bead #9.

Pass your needle back through the accent bead and back through beads #2 and #3.

Note: you may want to pass through beads #2 and #6 instead.

Pass your needle back through the accent bead, down bead #10, and up bead #1.

Pass your needle back through the accent bead and bead #7.

Continue with four-bead herringbone.

Using these instructions as a guide, you should be able to figure out how to use this technique with any tubular stitch. Make sure that you have a secure connection and the accent beads are centered on the rope.

MATERIALS
- Beading thread
- Size 10 or 12 beading needle
- 11º seed beads
- 8º seed beads

COMBINING SIX-BEAD HERRINGBONE AND PEYOTE

This bracelet combines 11º and 8º seed beads in earth-toned colors.

1. Using the instructions from the Ndebele herringbone chapter, work six-bead tubular herringbone for five rounds.

2. With your thread coming out the first bead of a V pair, pick up one 8º and pass your needle down through the second bead of the V pair and up the first bead of the next V pair.

3. Pick up one 8º and pass your needle down the second bead of this V pair and up the first bead of the next V pair.

4. Pick up one 8º and pass your needle down the second bead of the V pair and up the first bead of the next V pair, which is, of course, the first V pair of this round.

5. Step up by passing your needle through the first 8º of this round. You are set up to work three-bead peyote.

6. Work three-bead peyote for four rows.

To reverse the process and return to herringbone:

7. With your thread coming out an 8º, pick up two 11ºs and pass your needle through the next 8º.

8. Pick up two 11º s and pass your needle through the next 8º.

9. Pick up two 11ºs and pass your needle through the next 8º, which is, of course, the first 8º from this round.

10. Step up into the first 11º of the first V pair to begin working six-bead herringbone once again. Work to your desired length and finish as desired.

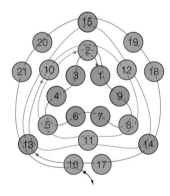

Combining six-bead herringbone and peyote

Here is another example of combining six-bead herringbone with tubular peyote using black and white 11º beads separated by brightly colored 8º and 11º beads.

Combining four-bead skinny herringbone with Peyote

This variation is done the same way as the six-bead bracelet on page 78. The difference is that you will be working with two pairs of beads for the herringbone and two beads for the peyote. Detailed instructions for skinny herringbone can be found in Chapter 8. If you look closely, you will see that I added a twisted-herringbone element to this bangle bracelet.

Combining skinny herringbone with two-bead peyote and herringbone increases

I could have included this lariat in Chapter 8, but because of the added peyote element, I chose to place it here. This lariat was worked from the center and stitched outward. I combined two-bead peyote near the ends and finished the ends with medium-sized Jasper briolettes. I used a bit of the herringbone increasing technique to hide the holes in the stones.

Diamond stitch II

If you ever invite me to your home for dinner, you can bet that I will show up at the door with something beaded and creatively wrapped as a thank you. This was the case when we were invited to a friend's home for a holiday party. With a limited amount of time to make something, I considered stitching a bangle bracelet using herringbone, or maybe one that combined herringbone with peyote. I was not sure, but as soon as I strung the first four beads, an idea hit me. The end result, shown here, has the look of another diamond-type stitch, but is done completely differently from the diamond stitch presented in Chapter 8. And the more I think about it, you can find this same type of variation in the peyote chapter under the increasing and decreasing section.

1. Using the 11º seed beads, stitch five rows using four-bead skinny herringbone.

2. With your needle coming up out the first V pair, pick up one 8º and pass your needle down through the second bead of the V pair to secure.

3. Pass your needle up through the first bead of the second V pair. Pick up one 8º and pass your needle down through the second bead of the V pair to secure. Finish the stitch by passing your needle up through the first bead of the adjacent V pair.

4. To begin the next row, step up by passing your needle through the first 8º.

5. Pick up two 11ºs and pass your needle through the second 8º.

6. Pick up two 11ºs and pass your needle through the first 8º again.

7. To begin the next row, pass your needle up through the first 11º of the first 11º pair.

8. Pick up one 8º and pass your needle down through the next 11º.

9. Skip the 8º and pass your needle up through the first bead of the next 11º pair.

10. Pick up one 8º and pass your needle down through the next 11º.

11. Skip over the 8º and pass your needle up through the first bead of the next 11º pair.

12. To begin the next row, step up by passing your needle through the first 8º.

13. Repeat **Steps 5–12** until you have completed a number of these rows.

14. Switch to regular herringbone as desired, alternating between the 8ºs and the 11ºs.

This stitch works up very quickly.

Peyote and brick stitch

In 2005, *Bead&Button* magazine published my article highlighting combined ruffled peyote and tubular brick stitch components. Over the past few years, I have had many nice comments about the components and have seen a number of designs made by other people using this technique. Not only are these components great strung together with other beads as spacers, but they also make wonderful toggle connectors that I use quite often. In order to make these, you will need a basic understanding of brick stitch (see Basics). To complete the ruffled tube to use as a toggle component, I have added large accent beads to each end.

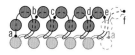

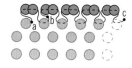

FIGURE 1

FIGURE 2

Ruffle

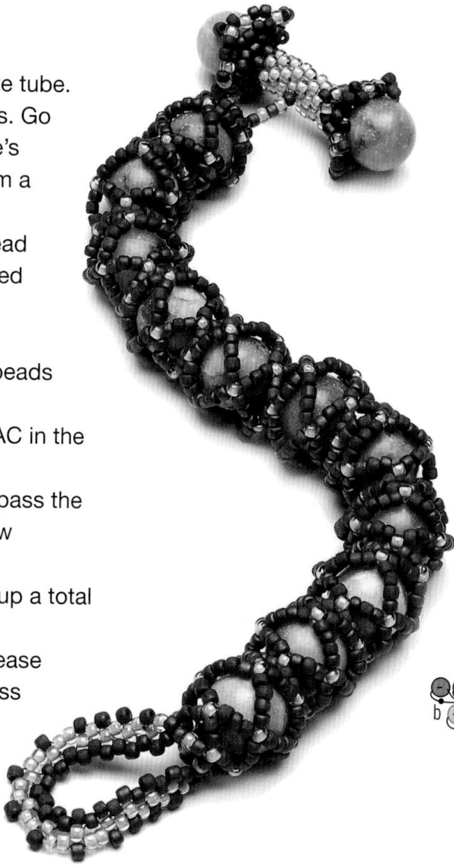

1. Make an eight-bead wide, 16 row peyote tube. Pick up three accent color (AC) seed beads. Go under the first thread bridge along the tube's edge and sew through the last bead to form a picot **(figure 1, a–b)**.

2. Pick up two ACs, go under the next thread bridge, and sew through the last bead added **(b–c)**.

3. Repeat **Step 2** twice **(c–d)**.

4. Pick up one AC **(d–e)**, for a total of ten beads added.

5. Pass the needle down through the first AC in the row, and through the first two ACs **(e–f)**.

6. Pick up two MCs (peyote increase) and pass the needle through the next AC on the picot row **(figure 2, a–b)**.

7. Repeat **Step 6** four more times, picking up a total of ten MCs **(b–c)**.

8. Step up through the first MC on the increase row **(figure 3, a–b)**. Pick up one AC and pass the needle through the next MC **(b–c)**. Repeat nine times, picking up a total of ten ACs **(c–d)**.

9. Step up through the first AC on the AC row **(figure 4, a–b)**. Pick up two MCs in every stitch across the row for a total of 20 MCs **(b–c)**.

10. Repeat **Step 8 (figure 5, a–b)**, picking up a total of 20 ACs **(b–c)**. Secure the thread.

11. Repeat on the other edge of the tube bead.

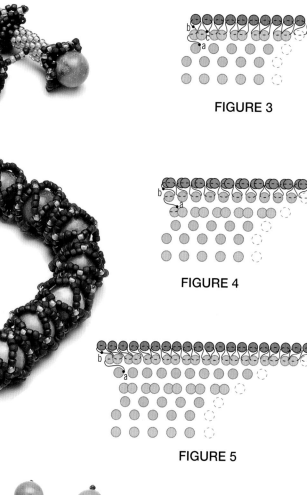

FIGURE 3

FIGURE 4

FIGURE 5

Skinny ropes

chapter **8**

Much of my "what-if" bead play ends up in a box, which I periodically give to my daughter Cheyenne to untangle. Once she is done, I stare at the untangled pieces and try to remember just what I did to create them. I ask myself constantly, "why couldn't I just write it all down as I went along?" "Next time," is usually my answer.

SKINNY ROPES

One of my play sessions led me to these four-bead skinny herringbone ropes. Sitting on my bead table was a plastic lanyard key chain that one of my daughters made me at camp (I guess you are never too old to play with lanyard). I really like the look of the lanyard with alternating colors and wondered if something similar could be created with beads. I was in a tubular herringbone mood so that is the stitch I used. The six-bead tubular ropes are round and fat, and I wanted something thinner and more square. I decided to try using just four beads to start. As I worked this rope exactly what I hoped for happened. I have since made a number of bangle bracelets like this. I need to offer a suggestion here, however. As cute as these are (especially a few worn together), they may not hold up very well over time as you roll them on and off your wrist. If I may be so bold, I would suggest using a small closure that will be a bit more durable.

PROJECT

MATERIALS
- Beading thread
- Size 10 or 12 beading needle
- 11° seed beads, matte black
- 11° seed beads, opaque turquoise

HERRINGBONE BRACELET

At the end of this project I will show you how to seamlessly connect the two ends to make a bangle. A warning: This technique is very addicting.

The following bracelet project using this four-bead herringbone technique works up very quickly.

Important note! If you wish to make your bracelet into a bangle, make very sure that you do not split the thread as you are beginning, as you later take the first thread round out of the beads.

a

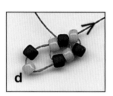
b

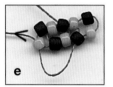
c

d

e

1. Pick up one black bead, one turquoise bead, one black, and one turquoise **(a)**.

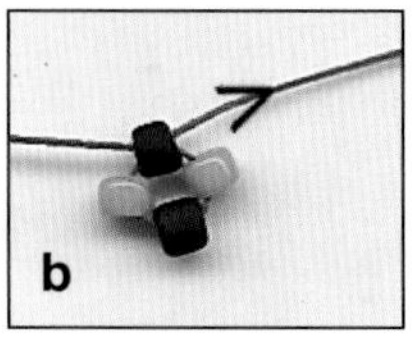

2. Create a circle of beads by passing your needle back through the first black bead in the direction you strung it **(b)**.

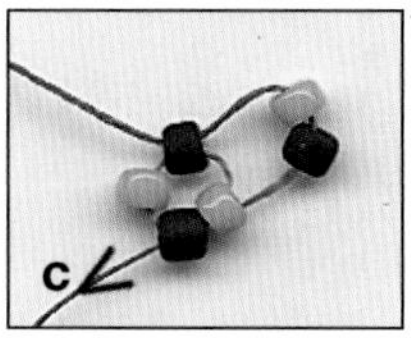

3. Pick up one turquoise bead and one black bead. Pass your needle through the next turquoise bead and the following black bead **(c)**.

4. Pick up one turquoise bead and one black bead. Pass your needle through the next turquoise bead and the following black bead. Because you now need to do a step up, you will need to also pass your needle through the next turquoise bead **(d)**.

5. Pick up one black bead and one turquoise bead. Pass your needle through the first black bead only. Refer back to the instructions for the regular tubular herringbone. You will now start to form the tube. Skip over the turquoise bead and the black bead. Pass your needle through the turquoise bead. This will put you in position to begin the next stitch **(e or figure 1)**. (Note: The excess thread will be pulled tight and will not show as you form the tube.)

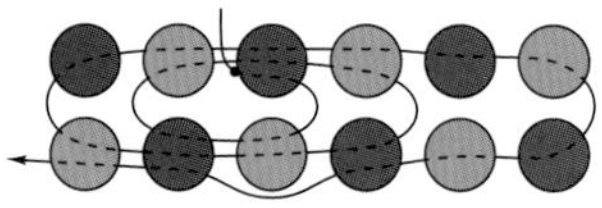

FIGURE 1

6. Pick up one black bead and one turquoise bead. Pass your needle through the black bead as shown **(figure 2)** .

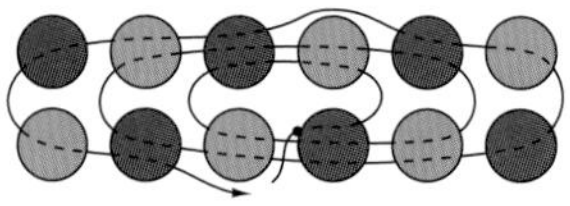

FIGURE 2

7. To begin the next round, you will need to step up by passing your needle through the turquoise bead and the black bead **(figure 3)**.

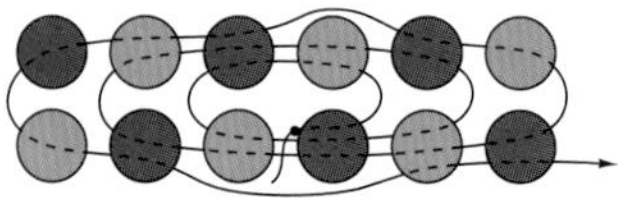

At this point you can now pull the beads into a tube. Once you have pulled the thread, you will be able to see the two sets of V columns. Continue working in this four-bead tubular herringbone technique until you reach your desired length.

FIGURE 3

If you wish to create a bangle bracelet, here are the instructions for seamlessly connecting the two ends:

8. First, remove the thread that was used to create the base circle of beads. Look closely at the first four beads you wove. Carefully pull the tail thread out the first bead, then the second bead, third bead, and finally the fourth bead **(figure 4)**.

FIGURE 4

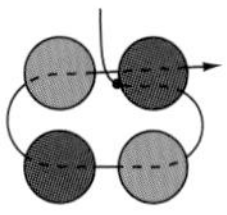

If you have done this correctly, you will have two pairs of bead columns that are not connected. And if you wanted to, you could continue beading the tube from this end.

Take a deep and cleansing breath because this is where it gets a bit tricky and possibly a bit frustrating. Make sure you can perfectly visualize how you have been creating this stitch. Here it is in a nutshell: With your needle coming out the top bead of a two-bead V column, pick up two beads. Secure those beads by passing your needle down through the second bead of the V pair. Pass your needle up through the first bead of the next two-bead V column, pick up two beads, pass your needle down the second bead of the V pair, and then do a step up by passing your needle through the top two beads of the next bead column.

Before connecting the two ends, straighten out the rope, making sure that you are connecting opposite colors to ensure a seamless finish. If not, you will need to stitch one more row.

9. Hold the two ends together and make sure it looks like **(figure 5)**. The bead holes will be facing each other. Your needle and thread will be coming out black bead #1 and your tail thread will be coming out turquoise bead #2 **(figure 6)**.

FIGURE 5

You are going to have think a little differently now because the beads that you would normally pick up for the next stitch are on the other end of the tube.

With your needle coming out black bead #1, pass your needle up through turquoise bead #2 and back down black bead #3. Secure this by passing your needle through bead #4.

FIGURE 6

You are halfway there.

Take a breath. Make sure that the tail thread is not crisscrossed with the working thread.

To continue...

Pass your needle through black bead #5. Pass your needle up through turquoise bead #6 and back down black bead #7. To secure, pass your needle through turquoise bead #8. To finish, pass your needle back through black bead #1 (in the direction toward bead #2).

It will look a little floppy right now but not for long.

The two threads should meet from opposite directions between beads #1 and #2. Make sure that the threads are not tangled.

Carefully tie an overhand knot and gently pull the threads until all the beads line up and you have a seamless connection.

Tie another knot.

Secure the tails in the work, making sure to tie little knots as you go.

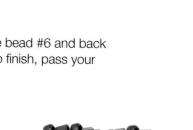

This bracelet uses 15º, 11º, and 8º seed beads blended with triangle beads and 8º hex beads.

Congratulations—you did it. Now I can rest.

However...

If congratulations are not in order due to a mistake somewhere, please do not scream, throw the book, call me names, or swear that there must be a typo somewhere. Gently take the thread out and start again. You will get it. Practice makes perfect. Look at the figures to get a good spatial understanding of how you are connecting the two ends. Start over, making sure that the bead holes are all facing each other before beginning the connection. Remember, when the going gets tough, the tough add a button, glass or stone bead, or toggle clasp instead. And it looks just fine.

Now that you know how to create a seamless connection, the possibilities are endless.

And speaking of possibilities...

I am always amazed at what happens to beadwork when different bead sizes are used in a project.

What if instead of using only 11ºs I also used 15ºs?

The result surprised me a bit. As I worked, I noticed that the larger beads started to naturally arc around the smaller beads. Yes, you can create a circle using just 11ºs (as shown in the previous bangle bracelet project) but remember that using two sizes of beads is part of the playtime that allows you to see what happens with different bead sizes.

After working for about 28 rows, I was able to comfortably connect the two ends. After connecting the ends, I decided that it looked boring, so I stitched a row of beads on the outside of the circle, which opened the door to so much potential.

As you work this stitch with two different bead sizes you can also create a long rope that has natural coil effect.

Coil variation

I made a number of these circles and wondered what to do with them.

The obvious answer was to connect them into a chain, but I wanted a less obvious idea so I contacted my new friend, Suzanne Golden, to ask her what she would do. Within moments she sent me a very rough drawing (she is laughing at that) of a necklace idea. Considering the number of circles I would have to make in order to create it was just not something I was going to do. Seems Suzanne is not afraid of long-term, complicated projects. Me, I like quick!

Another idea she had was to stack them and use them as a pendant. Definitely doable, I thought to myself, but as I worked my mind started to wander and then my hands started creating something else using the circles. This component is made up of two embellished circles stitched together and embellished a second time. I just like looking at it. And before you ask, I'll tell you that I don't remember exactly how I made it. But here it is. Maybe it will inspire you to play and see where you get.

Eventually, I went back to my more obvious idea of making a chain. I made three tiny circles, connected them, and realized that I was not ever going to make enough of these for a bracelet. So I stopped at three and decided to call it art.

I know if I look at these circles long enough an idea will come to me. Sure, they are perfect as toggle clasps, but what else? What would you do with them?

RUSSIAN SPIRAL

I would like to revisit a stitch I introduced in *Bead&Button* magazine and then in *Seed Bead Stitching*—the Russian spiral.

A story....

When I first presented the Russian spiral in *Bead&Button* I did not realize that it is actually a netting stitch. I did not pay much attention to how the stitch was formed. I just added beads as I saw fit and watched a fat rope of spiraling beads take shape. I made a number of these ropes and loved to see how different beads created such different looks both in pattern and in texture. As I was deciding which stitches to use for this book, I started playing with a netting stitch called the Ogalala butterfly, which is traditionally a flat stitch. My experiments with working with it in the round led me to understand just how the Russian spiral is formed. I realized that the placement of the beads determines the look of the spiral. Simply by changing the order of the beads, you change the look of the stitch.

The first rope is simply a skinny version of the original Russian spiral stitch. The second variation uses the same concept but changes the order of the beads. The end result is a stitch I call the diamond stitch because when you look at the rope from the side, the beads fall into what looks like little diamond shapes. Although it may resemble the diamond stitch created using peyote, it is different.

PROJECT

MATERIALS
- Beading thread
- Size 10 or 12 beading needle
- 11º seed beads
- 8º seed beads

SKINNY RUSSIAN SPIRAL

1. Pick up two 11ºs, one 8º , two 11ºs, and one 8º. Pass your needle back through the first 11º to create a circle. Your working thread and tail thread should be coming out the same bead in opposite directions **(a)**.

2. Pick up one 8º and two 11ºs. Skip the next 11º and 8ºs on the base ring of beads and pass your needle through the next 11º **(b)**.

3. Pick up one 8º and two 11ºs. Skip the next 11º and 8ºs on the base ring and pass your needle through the next 11º **(c)**.

4. To begin the next round you will need to step up by passing your needle through the 8º and the 11º **(d)**.

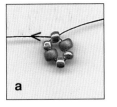

a

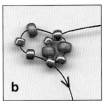

b

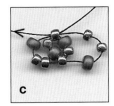

c

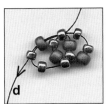

d

Note that your needle is coming out the center bead of the three beads that were added in **Step 2**. You will always pick up three new beads and then pass your needle through the center bead of the three-bead group added previously. Do this twice and then step up to begin the next round.

An easy way to think about it is that you will always pass your needle through the 11º immediately following the 8º.

At this point you should be able to start forming a bead tube. (My photos show the work flat to show the next thread path.)

e

5. Pick up one 8º and two 11ºs. Pass your needle through the 11º following the next 8º **(e)**.

Continue adding beads in this manner until you have reached your desired length.

Here is what a length of the rope will look like.

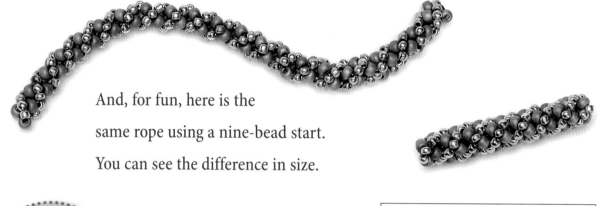

And, for fun, here is the
same rope using a nine-bead start.
You can see the difference in size.

PROJECT

MATERIALS
- Beading thread
- Size 10 or 12 beading needle
- 11º seed beads, red
- 11º seed beads, yellow
- 8º seed beads, turquoise

SUPER-SKINNY RUSSIAN SPIRAL

I have shown how to create a regular Russian spiral using a nine-bead start and a skinny Russian spiral using a six-bead start, but what about a super skinny Russian spiral using a three-bead start? Would that even be possible to do? Let's find out.

My first attempt worked out beautifully—exactly as I had hoped. You have made it to Chapter 8 of my second book, so I feel fairly comfortable suggesting that you do not try this variation if you are having a stressful day or moment. The first two rounds might put you over the edge as you try to keep them straight. Then, after all of your work to try to keep it straight, I am going to tell you to remove two of the beads.

Okay, you have been warned. Now let's have some fun.

For demonstration purposes, I used two different 11º bead colors. Once you get the hang of this variation, you will be able to easily use just one 11º color if you wish.

1. Pick up one red bead, one yellow bead, and one turquoise bead. Create a circle by passing your needle back through the first red bead. The working thread and tail thread should be coming out the same red bead in opposite directions. Make sure that you do not split the thread since you will be removing the yellow and turquoise beads from the finished rope **(a)**.

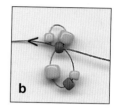

2. Pick up one turquoise bead, one red bead, and one yellow bead. Create a second circle of beads by again passing your needle through the red bead from the base round **(b)**.

As you begin this rope, use the yellow and turquoise beads from the base round to hold onto your work.

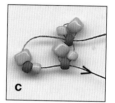

3. Pick up one turquoise bead, one red bead, and one yellow bead. Holding onto the yellow and turquoise beads from the base row for support, pass your needle through the red bead **(c)**.

As you pull the thread tight, make sure that the new beads are sitting on top of the old beads.

Continue holding the yellow and turquoise beads for support as you pick up one turquoise bead, one red bead, and one yellow bead. Pass your needle through the red bead next to the turquoise bead from the previous row.

After you have completed a few rows, you can pull out the yellow and turquoise beads from the base row, since you will no longer need them for support. Keep working until you feel comfortable with the stitch.

Here is a picture of a finished length of rope using the same beads as the other two Russian spiral variations.

DIAMOND STITCH

The stitch I call the diamond stitch and the Russian spiral are actually the same stitch. The difference is the placement of the beads. How cool is that? The two lariat necklaces on page 56 use this stitch. Each uses only two different beads throughout. I played with the patterns. Sometimes I used one bead for all of the centers and other times I used the other bead for the center. Sometimes I used one bead for one round and the other bead for the next round.

PROJECT

MATERIALS
- Beading thread
- Size 10 or 12 beading needles
- 11º seed beads, purple
- 11º seed beads, green

Create your own unique patterns and textures. I know you can come up with some amazing combinations.

DIAMOND STITCH ROPE

Here are the stitch basics using two contrasting 11º seed beads.

a

1. Pick up eight beads, alternating purple and green and beginning with a purple. Create a circle by passing your needle back through the first purple bead in the same direction you strung it. Your working thread and tail thread should be coming out the same bead in opposite directions **(a)**.

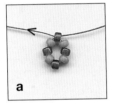
b

2. With your thread coming out the top purple bead, pick up one green, one purple, and one green. Connect to the work by passing your needle through the bottom purple **(b)**.

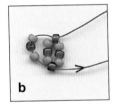
c

3. With your needle coming out the bottom purple, pick up one green, one purple, and one green. Connect to the work by passing your needle through the top purple. Your working thread and tail thread will be coming out the same bead in opposite directions **(c)**.

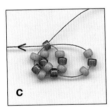
d

4. Time to step up. Remember that this is a tube, so even though my work is shown flat, your work is not going to be. The beads you strung for the base row will, of course, sit under the new beads you just added in **Steps 2 and 3**. You will need to step up into the first two beads you added in **Step 2**, the green bead and the purple bead.

Pull the beads into the beginning of a tube **(d)**.

The whole premise of this stitch is that it is a form of netting. For each stitch, you pick up three beads and attach them to the center bead of a three-bead set from the previous row. Do this twice and then step up.

e

Once you get the hang of the stitch (same as the Russian spiral, just a different order of beads) you can start playing with other bead combinations and patterns.

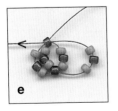

This wonderful rope sampler uses my favorite technique of color-blocking using beads of different shapes, colors, and sizes.

MATERIALS
- Beading thread
- Size 10 or 12 beading needle
- 11º seed beads, green
- 11º seed beads, purple
- 8º seed beads
- 6º seed beads

BONUS: SQUARE PILLOWS

I don't know about you, but I seem to amass many containers filled with beads, fondly known as bead soup, left over from past projects. I had an idea one night to make a striped herringbone stitched bracelet using some of these beads. After finding four identical beads, I began the bracelet. I quickly realized I would have the patience to search for beads for about 10 rows. Still wanting to use some of these beads (OK, truth be told, I added some of my favorite beads to the mix before I started), I started playing. Before I knew it, I had this cute little square pillow bead in my hand.

The possibilities of how to use these are endless: earrings, pendants, bracelets …

Because these little pillow beads don't really fit into any one chapter in this book, I thought it would be fun to add them as a bonus project. I love bonus stuff, don't you?

These cute beaded beads can be made in a very short time. The two sides can be identical or different. Can you imagine the number of color combinations? Grab just a few beads and get started.

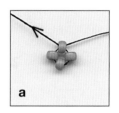
a

b

c

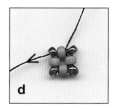
d

1. String four 11º green beads. Create a circle by passing your needle back through the first bead in the same direction you strung it. Your working thread and tail thread should be coming out the same bead in opposite directions **(a)**.

2. Pick up one 11º purple bead. Pass your needle through the next green bead **(b)**.

3. Repeat **Step 2** three times. Your working thread and tail thread should be coming out the same bead in opposite directions **(c)**.

4. Step up by passing your needle through the first purple bead **(d)**.

5. Pick up two 8°s and pass your needle through the next purple bead **(e)**.

6. Pick up two 8°s and pass your needle through the next purple bead three more times. Be sure to step up into the first 8° to begin the next round **(f)**.

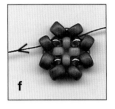

7. Pick up one 6° bead and pass your needle through the next two 8°s **(g)**.

8. Repeat **Step 7** three times. Step up into the first 6° to begin the next round **(h)**.

9. Pick up four green beads and pass your needle through the next 6° **(i)**.

10. Repeat **Step 9** three times **(j)**.

Do not step up!

You are now going to reverse the process and create the back of the pillow. The four 11° green beads that you just added are the midpoint of this piece. Notice that when you pull your thread tight, the beads begin to cup. Make sure that this cup is turned up so that the new beads you are adding will be worked toward the open center.

11. Pick up two 8°s and pass your needle through the next 6°. Make sure these beads are sitting on top of the cup and not underneath it.

12. Repeat **Step 11** three times.

13. Pass your needle up through the first 8° bead to begin the next round.

14. Pick up one 11° purple bead and pass your needle through the next two 8°s.

15. Repeat **Step 14** three times.

16. Pick up one 11° green bead and pass your needle through the next purple bead.

17. Repeat **Step 16** three times.

18. Tighten the beads on the innermost round by circling your thread through the beads several times. Weave your tail thread and working thread in and out the beads. Secure the thread.

Tah dah! Little beaded pillow beads.

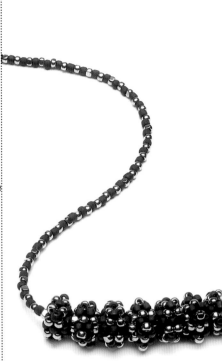

Toggle components

Short sections of the technique used for the bracelets will make very nice toggle clasp components (below).

Or you can string a short section as the focal point of a short necklace as shown here using 11° matte black and 11° hex-cut silver beads.

MATERIALS
• Beading thread
• Size 10 or 12 beading needle
• 11º seed beads

SQUARE PILLOW BRACELETS

These bracelets are a variation of the square pillow technique. They are also a variation of peyote increases and decreases. Instead of ending each section, I used the end of each element as the base for the next one. If you refer to Chapter 4, which taught you to add layers to the triangles and squares, you will understand how these bracelets are formed.

1. Using all 11ºs, follow the first six steps from the square pillows instructions.

2. Add one 11º between each 11º from the previous round. You will have eight protruding beads at the end of this round.

3. Work three more rows of peyote. At the end of this round, step up into the first two protruding beads to begin the next row.

4. Add one 11º and pass through the next two 11ºs. Add one 11º and pass through the next two 11ºs. Add one 11º and pass through the next two 11ºs. Add one 11º and pass through the two 11ºs you stepped up into to begin this round. Notice that you now have four protruding beads. Step up into the first of these four beads to begin the next round.

5. Pick up one 11º and pass through the next protruding 11º. Pick up one 11º and pass your needle through the next protruding 11º. Repeat two more times. To finish this round, you will need to pass your needle through the last four beads that you added in this round a couple of times.

Use these four beads as the base for the next element.

You will notice that the elements in this bracelet are a bit varied. I changed the size of beads and number of rounds of beads to see what would happen.

To make a seamless connection, make half an element on each end and then zip them up. After some trial and error, I found that this is the easiest way to do it—trust me.

MY THOUGHTS

Art is much less important than life, but what a poor life without it.

~Robert Motherwell

It is Tuesday, November 11, 2008. Our country has just elected a new president who has filled us with hope. People are praying for their jobs, their homes, their families, and their loved ones in the armed services. Yet here I sit, quietly beading, alone with my thoughts.

My daughter Cheyenne is studying for a test and my daughter Sierra is preparing for the biggest audition of her young life. Yet here I sit, quietly beading alone with my thoughts. My dog is resting, my husband is working, and here I sit, quietly beading, alone with my thoughts. With everything going on around me, I feel peaceful. That's what creatively beading does for me. It gives me peace. It makes me smile. And really, it gives me something to do besides laundry and housework.

Shortly after I agreed to write this book I worried that I had bitten off more than I could chew. But then, I dove into the work I love so much and I got into a rhythm. The hours flew by each day. I didn't want to stop even when I knew that the girls were waiting to be picked up, that dinner had to be cooked, and that darn laundry needed to be folded. I don't dare mention the layers of dust, but I've decided that living with a dusty house was actually part of the fun of writing a book. It's a built-in excuse. And really, I have two teenage girls who can help me. Yeah, right. But I digress.

I know people are keeping their hard-earned money close these days, and not necessarily running out to buy that one-of-a-kind hand-crafted piece of beaded art. They are, however, ready, willing, and able to learn how to do it themselves. Getting started does not have to be expensive. You only need a few tubes of beads, some needles, and thread. The rest is up to you.

I truly love beading. I learn new things every time I sit down to work. I even learned a few new things while writing this book. One idea seems to always lead me to another. As I worked each stitch, I discovered things that I just had to share.

Now, it's time for a shower and lunch with some friends. I might even cook dinner for a change. Thank you for allowing me to be your teacher and your bead friend as you begin or continue your own creative journey.

Much love,

Beth

In case you're wondering, Cheyenne got an A. And Sierr role of Millie in *Thoroughly Modern Millie*.

ABOUT THE AUTHOR

Beth's first love is seed bead work—creating art by combining tiny points of color using different off-loom bead-stitching techniques. In addition to her seed bead work, she also creates one-of-a-kind and limited edition bracelets and necklaces using vintage and new glass, sterling silver, freshwater pearls, and gemstones. Completely self-taught, Beth says her mistakes are often her best lessons. Beth has shown her work at art shows since 1990 and has had her work displayed and sold in a number of fine-art galleries and gift stores. She was first published in *Bead&Button* in 1998 and since then has been featured numerous times in magazines and books from Kalmbach Publishing Co. She lives in West Bloomfield, Mich., with her husband, two daughters, and dog.

THANK YOU TO ...

My beloved husband, Sheldon. Thank you for your never ending love, for the moon, and for telling me that the dust is "no big deal." I love you forever.

Cheyenne and Sierra. You inspire me every day to be the best I can be. Even on days when I am not. I love you both more than you know.

My mom, Ina Katz, and my sister, Lori Silverstein. As always, thank you for a lifetime of love, laughter, and support.

Kalmbach Books. Thank you for allowing me to continue to share what I love.

Karin Buckingham. You are a wonderful editor and friend. I love the book and can't thank you enough for taking care of my baby as though it were one of your own.

Mary Wohlgemuth. Thank you for the idea for the tubular herringbone increasing and decreasing necklace. How 'bout those instructions?

Cissy Gast. Once again, I cannot thank you enough for all of the encouragement, support, e-mails, editing, and instruction testing. You make me smile even when we disagree.

Suzanne Golden. You are an incredible artist and inspiration for so many. Thank you for your kind words, for sharing your thoughts and for all of the fun e-mails.

The wonderfully creative artists who shared a part of themselves with me and the readers of this book. I can't thank you enough for your ideas, thoughts, and inspirations. It was pleasure to include you all.

My friends. Thank you for all you do to encourage me to reach higher.

The readers and beaders who were so generous with their words of praise for my first book. I hope you enjoy this one and continue to find inspiration on your bead journey.

SOURCES

Some of my very favorite bead stores:

Priya Imports, Inc.
248.851.3400
Priyaimportsinc.com
priyaimports@earthlink.net

T & T Trading, Inc.
1063 E Grand Ledge Highway
Grand Ledge, MI 48837
517.627.2333
tttbeads.com

Brighton Beads and More
9850 Grand River
Brighton, MI 48116
810.844.0066
brightonbeadsandmore.com

Beadies Beadwork
19985 Westover Avenue
Rocky River, OH 44116
beadiesbeadwork.com
beadies@beadiesbeadwork.com
Linda, thanks for the beads!!

The Beadin' Path ®
15 Main Street
Freeport, ME 04032
877.92BEADS
International: 207.865.4785
beadinpath.com

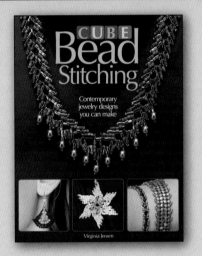
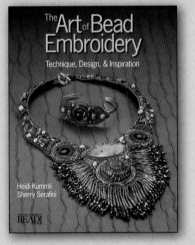